THE O+ PLUS FACTOR

Overcoming Obstacles on the Road to Success

Angela D. Akers

Seven Worlds Corporation
Knoxville, Tennessee

Printed in the United States of America

Library of Congress Catalog Card Number: 98-61618

ISBN: 0-936497-49-1

All scripture is taken from the Revised Standard Version of the Bible.

Cover design by Cheri Jorgenson, Cheri Jorgenson Design, Knoxville, Tennessee

Seven Worlds Corporation
310 Simmons Rd.
Knoxville, Tennessee 37922
800-848-5547

CONTENTS

THIS BOOK IS DEDICATED TO
MY WONDERFUL HUSBAND,
BILL, WHO HAS TAUGHT ME SO
MUCH ABOUT OVERCOMING.

Introduction

I was two years old the first time it happened. My two older sisters and I were watching Saturday morning cartoons when I started shaking all over. I didn't respond when my sisters called my name. So they ran to get my parents. Imagine their horror when they saw their toddler daughter wracked by strange convulsions. At the hospital, I was diagnosed with a rare but potentially fatal form of epilepsy.

The next fifteen years would be terrifying for my parents and frustrating for me. They never knew when, in the dark of night, they would hear the tell-tale thrashing on the other side of the wall that indicated I was locked in convulsions. I never knew when I went to bed each night if I would wake up in my own room the next morning, or if I would wake up in a hospital bed, surrounded by strangers. But the worst part was not the occasional seizures which were, mercifully, few and far between. The worst part was the heavy medication required to control my condition. I thank God for that medication. But while it held the seizures at bay, it exacted a high price in return. The medicine left me foggy, forgetful, depressed. I often felt as if life were a party to which I wasn't invited. I was just sharp enough to realize that I was not as smart as everyone else. I had trouble concentrating in school, and often suffered horrible headaches. Even though my mother tutored me every day after school, I was a mediocre student, at best. Some teachers tried to shame me by reminding me of my sisters' accomplishments. I cried often, and retreated into my imagination. When the doctors tinkered with my medication, I became even more hazy. I walked into walls, forgot where my classes were, and became, in the words of my older sister, a "zombie."

My freshman year of college, I celebrated five years without any seizures. The doctors decided to end my medication. Little did I know how profoundly my life would change.

I remember one very special day: I was sitting down to study for my first big exam in Old Testament theology. With endless pages of notes to memorize by 8:00 the next morning, I planned to study for at least six hours. But after two hours of intense concentration, I needed a snack break. As I closed my books, a stream of Bible facts ran through my mind. Covenants, definitions, religious laws—I could see it all as if I were running a movie reel in my head. Wait a minute! I'd only been studying two hours. How did I know all this information? I opened my books again and reviewed the material. I knew it. All of it.

It was like a door had opened up in my mind and suddenly I had access to new areas of thought and learning. Learning became easy for me. Memorizing became easy for me. So much that had been difficult before suddenly became easy for me. Except believing in myself. For so many years, I had thought of myself as the dumb one in the family. I had been the one who needed extra help in school. I had been the one the teachers clucked over. And now, in a span of a few months' time, I had become "smart." My grades reflected it. My self-image didn't. Years of shame and self-doubt had accumulated like scar tissue over a wound. It would take many years before I learned to believe in myself. Until I developed that confidence, I could not take charge of my life.

We all have some obstacle in life, something that keeps us from reaching our full potential. On the pages of this book, you will meet people who have overcome the worst imaginable obstacles on the road to success. You will read stories of childhood abuse, physical disabilities, poverty, failure, poor self-image. Sounds like a downer? No way, *mis amigos*. You see, every story has a happy ending. Every person in this book overcame his or her obstacle in order to find success and fulfillment. These people are unique because they found a way to transcend their past, their circumstances, or their limitations.

In studying these stories, I've found a cluster of characteristics that seem to mark the lives of overcomers:

> † *an unquenchable passion*
> † *a dose of self-confidence*
> † *a network of encouragers*
> † *a disregard for limits*
> † *acquisition of important skills*
> † *a commitment to significance*
> † *and a faith in God.*

All these elements combine to make up what I call the O+ Plus Factor. And you can access the O+ Plus Factor in your life. I don't know what obstacles you may be facing, but I do know that you are worthy of reaching your highest potential. By reading this book, you are choosing to make an investment in yourself. Who knows what returns you'll receive? You may see obstacles in your own life fall away as you face up to them with faith, confidence, and commitment. My prayer is that these stories will inspire you to overcome your own past, circumstances, or limitations and to reach for your highest, God-given potential.

Many years ago, the Cherokee population in the United States was largely illiterate. There was no written Cherokee language; only verbal communication was possible. Then Sequoyah, a Cherokee brave, was badly injured in a hunting accident. His injuries left him unable to participate in common activities like hunting and games. With so much extra time on his hands, Sequoyah began experimenting with a written language. He analyzed the speech of those around him, and created symbols to represent each sound. He went off by himself for hours at a time to work on his strange drawings. Soon, other members of Sequoyah's tribe began to mock him.

After twelve years of experimentation, Sequoyah finally developed a written alphabet of the Cherokee language. It was so simple to learn that knowledge of this alphabet spread throughout the Cherokee population in the United States. Sequoyah became a hero to his people.

1

BE PASSIONATE!

Go After Your

Dreams

C an you remember the day a dream really took hold of you? Clay Whitehurst of Brentwood, Tennessee, can. In fact, he knows the exact date: October 28, 1977. Clay was in the sixth grade when he decided that he wanted to play football for the University of Alabama, the Crimson Tide. What sparked this ambitious dream? A few simple words of encouragement.

Clay was a naturally athletic kid who worked hard at sports. In the sixth grade, he was playing for a local boys' football team in Brentwood. Clay's coach was a friend of Bear Bryant, the outstanding coach at Alabama. Clay's coach told his friend about Clay, and so Bear Bryant wrote the boy a letter full of encouragement and gentle advice on putting forth as much effort in school as in football. He ended the letter by saying that he hoped Clay would grow up to play for Alabama someday. Clay received that letter on October 28, 1977, and his dream was set from that day on. He collected Alabama paraphernalia. He watched every Alabama game on TV, and he worked hard to develop into an outstanding athlete.

After high school, Clay Whitehurst was offered scholarships to many different schools, but he chose the University of Alabama.

He had an excellent career as a wide receiver for the Crimson Tide, maintaining a spot as a starting player all four years in college. He achieved his dream, a dream sparked by nothing more than a few well-timed, encouraging words.

Have a passion. Every life needs a passion, a dream or goal that is unique to the dreamer. This is one area where "comparisonitis" is deadly. You are a wholly unique mixture of thoughts, impulses, influences, experiences, and abilities. Your passions are no less special. Give yourself permission to be outrageous. Heck, you can't get much more outrageous than John Searing, an arts-supplies salesman from New Jersey.

John Searing's one great goal in life was to yell, "He-e-e-ere's Johnny!" on "The Tonight Show." He had been a fan of the show for years, and in 1980 John wrote to the show and asked for the chance to fill in for Ed, just for one night. He received an autographed picture in reply. That didn't faze John Searing. For the next six years, he wrote over 800 letters to "The Tonight Show." Searing even sent audio tapes of himself doing impersonations of various stars.

Finally, John's persistence paid off. He was invited to California, where "The Tonight Show" staff ferried him around in a limousine, and Johnny Carson himself interviewed John on his strange obsession. And then, John was placed in front of a microphone and allowed to do the introduction. Drum roll and all. John Searing fulfilled his passion.

Now that's a man on fire! Who could possibly say no to tenacity like that? Not me. Maybe you and I don't share John Searing's passion for late-night TV. So what? We've got to admire the man who refuses to let his passions petrify into passivity. One of the best ways to stay engaged in life is to **let your enthusiasm spill over**. Enthusiasm may not be cool or sophisticated. It's childlike. It's letting down your defenses and exposing your heart to the world. A perfect example of this type of childlike enthusiasm can be found in the story of Luke Zimmerman.

Luke, a Down's syndrome student in special classes at Beverly Hills High School, is fanatical about his school's football team. When Beverly Hills coach Carter Paysinger met Luke, he was impressed by the boy's love of the game. Paysinger invited Luke to become the team manager. He came to all the workouts and helped out on the field. After one particular game, Luke gave an impassioned, go-get-'em speech that inspired the players, and became a team tradition.

Occasionally, Coach Paysinger will even put Luke in for a few plays. His enthusiasm out on the field fires up both teams. Luke Zimmerman is an example to them of someone who has achieved a dream against mighty odds.

Where does passion come from? We first recognize our passions when we are children. Children naturally understand passion (defined here as an intense emotion or eager desire). They live life to the fullest. They feel every emotion deeply. When I play peek-a-boo with my little nephew, Sebastian, he throws his head back and squeals with laughter. The word *moderation* is not in his vocabulary. (One could note that, at his tender age, lots of words are not in my nephew's vocabulary. In fact, Sebastian's current vocabulary consists of the words "Mama," "hot," "no!," and various animal noises, but you get the point.) My niece, Rachel, wants to be, do, and try everything. She sees life as one giant frontier waiting to be explored. Children believe that life is without limits. They want to experience everything. As Dr. J.A. Holmes once said, "Never tell a young person that something cannot be done. God may have been waiting for centuries for somebody ignorant enough of the impossibility to do that thing."

From Pain to Passion

Sometimes a passion can be fueled by heartbreak, by adversity. Sometimes, you have to dream in spite of . . .

In 1969, Jan Scruggs came home from the Vietnam War with a body wounded by shrapnel and a heart scarred by tragedy. He dreamed of creating some sort of monument to the soldiers who suffered through one of America's most contentious wars. But he had no money and no idea how to get started.

In 1979, Jan was stirred to action by the movie *The Deer Hunter*, a story about the war's effect on a group of friends. He established the Vietnam Veterans Memorial Fund and began spreading the word and gathering support. The federal government donated a plot of land and gave Jan a deadline of five years to use it. Within two years, he had raised enough money to break ground on a monument.

On November 13, 1982, Jan Scruggs attended the dedication services for the Vietnam Veterans Memorial. How many men and women veterans of the Vietnam War have found healing by visiting this memorial? How many lives have been touched by Jan Scruggs' passion?

Jan Scruggs' story teaches us a valuable lesson: **Overcomers know that true passion cannot be extinguished by pain.** Pain is a natural part of life, and it is only one's response to heartbreak and adversity that matters.

In 1944, one of Sweden's premier equestriennes, Lis Hartel, contracted the dread disease, polio. Paralysis set in quickly. Though her doctor warned Lis that she might never walk again unaided, she threw herself wholeheartedly into physical therapy. Hour upon hour, day upon day, Lis fought through the pain and frustration involved in rehabilitating her legs. Lis' mother and husband also devoted themselves to her healing. The dressage event, Lis' forte, involves guiding a horse through subtle movements of the leg muscles. It requires intense concentration and great physical skills.

By 1947, just three years after contracting polio, Lis Hartel was once again riding dressage. A look back in an old sports almanac will show you that Lis Hartel of Stockholm, Sweden, won silver medals in the dressage event at both the 1952 and the 1956 Olympic Games.

What was Lis Hartel's response to adversity? *This town ain't big enough for the both of us . . . It's time for a showdown at the O.K. Corral . . . You better get the heck out of Dodge . . .* Okay, I've run out of tough-guy phrases from old Western movies. But you get the point. She didn't cave in. Her passion for riding was too overwhelming to be overcome by polio.

When people care that much for something, they find a way to accomplish it.

A little girl was born into poverty in rural Mississippi. In childhood, two near-fatal car accidents left her with serious injuries to her back and leg, and 100 stitches in her face. Doctors didn't think she'd ever walk again. When her cast came off, the healed leg was two inches shorter than the uninjured one. With determination and faith, she taught herself to walk again.

At the age of seventeen, the young woman's leg was miraculously healed, and a new dream was planted in her heart: to enter the Miss America competition. This poor, scarred girl from Mississippi believed that God was calling her to this goal. For five years, she entered and lost the pageant. But in 1980, Cheryl Prewitt was finally crowned Miss America. Today, Cheryl works in music and television, and has written a number of books, some best-sellers. At one time, Cheryl Prewitt's physical and emotional scars stood as towering obstacles deterring her from reaching her goals. But Cheryl learned a great lesson: scars are the mark of the overcomer. What separates the high achievers from the mediocrities is not a lack of adversity in life. It is what high achievers do with their adversity that leads them on to excellence.

13

The O+ Plus Factor

True passion leads to initiative, and initiative leads to direction, and direction leads to commitment, and commitment leads to triumph. Try saying that ten times fast!

Grand Adventures

Here's another overcomers' secret: **Having a passion leads to a much richer life.** At the age of 37, journalist Mike McIntyre decided to hitchhike across the country in the hopes of seeing what America and Americans are really like these days. Armed with only a backpack and a humble sign reading simply, "America," Mike set out on his adventure.

Mike reports that his whole trip was a lesson in the kindness of strangers. People gave him food, shelter, even a winter coat and a Bible.

At the end of his trip, Mike McIntyre realized that he had a new respect for his country and its people. As he wrote, ". . . it took giving up money to have the richest experience of my life. I knew that wherever I might go, I would always remember my continental leap of faith--and the country that caught me."

Don't you want an experience like that? One that will change your perspective, one that will really stir you?

In 1930, Amelia Earhart set the women's speed and altitude records in aviation. In 1932, she was the first woman to cross the Atlantic solo. But in 1937 she attempted her greatest feat, a 25,000 mile, round-the-world trip. It would have earned her a place in history. On July 2, 1937, Earhart's plane disappeared over Howland Island, just 3,000 miles short of her destination.

In 1997, a single mother named Linda Finch set out to re-create Amelia Earhart's trip around the world, exactly sixty years since Earhart's disappearance. At her various stops along the way, Finch spoke at schools. She hopes to teach children about aviation, and to inspire them to reach beyond their limits.

And when Linda Finch flew over Howland Island in the Pacific, she dropped a memorial wreath in honor of the woman who died in pursuit of a passion and an ideal.

Heady stuff, to be sure. Stories of adventurers set our hearts beating faster, but there is also an element of self-indulgence in their exploits. At this point, you might be saying to yourself, *"Wait a minute, Angela. All this 'exploring your passion' stuff sounds pretty selfish. You've left do, re, fa, so, la, ti out of the musical scale, and all you're singing is mi! Me, me, me!"* Forgive me, *mis amigos,* if I've given you the impression that this is a book about self-indulgence. Every great advancement in learning, in technology, in medicine, in social relations came about because somebody was pursuing a passion. Do you think Thomas Edison was thinking about you or me when he invented the light bulb? Henri Dunant's passion for eliminating human suffering led to the founding of the Red Cross.

Overcomers know the pursuit of their passion may very well enrich and improve the lives of others around them.

A great American inventor of the last century, Norbert Rillieux, was a former slave who worked in the sugar cane industry.

A daily task in the sugar industry involved sifting sugar cane juice from one pan to another to refine it. The juice reached scalding temperatures, and many people suffered serious burns from it. Some even died of their injuries. Norbert Rillieux took it upon himself to improve the process. He invented a vacuum evaporation pan that eliminated the need for sifting the sugar cane juice. His design was so revolutionary that it is still being used in the sugar and sugar beet industries today. Norbert Rillieux's sympathy for those men and women in the sugar-cane industry would not let him rest until he invented a mechanism to help. His passion alleviated the suffering of others.

Rich Walsh was a successful builder living in the dynamic city of Seattle, Washington, until the day a tragic car accident left him a quadriplegic. In the face of such a life-shattering event, most of us would be tempted to surrender to helplessness or self-pity. Instead, Rich Walsh turned his attention to helping others who are in his same predicament.

He established a training school for profoundly handicapped people. Rich's school, the Resource Center for the Handicapped, trains people to program and use computers in a variety of jobs, and many of his graduates have gone on to lucrative careers at high-powered technology firms in Seattle. Rich Walsh has used his own tragedy to enrich the lives of hundreds of other people. And he himself believes that the accident and its aftermath have allowed him to live a "life of significance." There is no selfishness in these mens' pursuit of their passion. They have contributed to the greater good of humanity.

No Regrets

Overcomers' lives are enriched by a simple truth that millions of unfulfilled people do not know: **Anything truly worth achieving is going to require commitment**.

How much blood, sweat, and tears is the human body capable of expending? Those who give their all to their passion will tell you that it is an almost limitless amount. One of the great things about having a passion is that it allows you to concentrate your energies. You are less wasteful with your time, talents, and resources. And often one's energy and determination increase in direct proportion to the size and "impossibility" of their dream.

Missionary C.T. Studd was on fire for God, willing to risk anything and go anywhere for the Lord he loved and served. When he planned to return to Africa to do missionary work, many around him warned that he would be killed, that he would become a martyr of the faith. Studd answered, "Praise God, I've just been looking for a chance to die for Jesus." What would our church or our society look like if all believers had that level of commitment? What would our schools, workplaces, homes look like if we all had a passion like that?

When you commit yourself to living your passion, you will know that you can look back without regrets.

The little girl was only ten years old when her mother died of cancer. As an adult, she reports, "I have a marker in my head of March 17, 1973. Everything in my memory is either before or after that date. After that date, my life was changed forever." The family never really talked about the mother's death. The little girl's father turned, instead, to drinking. The little girl escaped her sadness by immersing herself in movies and books. Also, she began to develop some of the burning ambition that would mark her adult life. She imagined that her mother had died with many unfulfilled dreams, so she resolved to achieve as much as possible in life. Her dramatic personality and quick wit have served her well. For this sad little girl grew up to be comedienne and talk-show host, Rosie O'Donnell.

Rosie O'Donnell is a wonderfully gifted young woman. But would she ever have realized her gifts to the extent that she has, if it were not for her desire to live without regrets? Do you really want to look back over your life and be confronted by a long list of "if only's"? Don't you wish that you were bolder, more concentrated, more committed, more reckless?

George O. Wood writes proudly of his aunt, Ruth Plymire, a valiant woman who spent her life ministering to the people of China and Tibet. One can only imagine the hardships, the frustrations,

> **Passion is useless without resolve. There is a turning point in overcomers' lives when they make the decision to follow their dreams no matter what.**

and the rejection she must have faced. She may never have known how many lives she affected, or if she even affected one. Yet she chose as the legend on her tombstone two triumphant words that sum up her life: "No regrets."

Do you want to live without regrets? Then figure out what you are passionate about and go for it. It is the first step in becoming an overcomer.

19

Overcomers' Secrets:

1. Have a passion.
2. Let your enthusiasm spill over.
3. True passion cannot be extinguished by pain.
4. Having a passion leads to a much richer life.
5. The pursuit of your passion may enrich the lives of others.
6. Anything worth achieving requires commitment.
7. Live your passion, and you can look back without regrets.

2

BELIEVE IN YOURSELF: Confidence for Dummies

In 1947, Bill Walsh was a proud, first-year member of
Fordham University's football team. But his coach, Vince
Lombardi, didn't see much potential in the young athlete.
He dropped Walsh from the team, telling him, "There's plenty you
do well, but football is not one of them." As you know, Vince
Lombardi went on to become one of professional football's most
successful coaches. His Green Bay Packers captured a stunning
five NFL titles, and secured Lombardi's place in history. Vince
Lombardi obviously knew a thing or two about football.

Happily, Bill Walsh figured out what things he could do well,
too. He went on to become a venture capitalist. A successful
venture capitalist. How successful? Well, in May 1997, William
D. Walsh donated $10 million to Fordham University's new
library. Oh, and he chipped in another $500,000 toward the
creation of an athletic training center.

Don't you love a story like that? There is something in us that
thrills to the success of others, especially when the journey of
success includes a few speed bumps along the way. Getting

21

dropped from the team must have been painful. It's so easy for us to let setbacks weasel their way into our souls. And, after a while, we become convinced that a weakness in one area of our lives reflects on other areas of our life. Taken to the extreme, our attitude of "Maybe I'm just no good *at* . . ."can subtly morph into "Maybe I'm just no good . . ."

I can relate to that attitude. As the third of four children in a family (all girls), I was often defined more by what I couldn't do than what I could do. I remember distinctly the day a woman in our church decided to introduce the four Duncan girls to a visitor. She pointed to my oldest sister, Rebecca, and said, "This is Rebecca. She's the smart one in the family. She gets such good grades." Next, she pointed to my older sister, Deborah. "And this is Deborah, the pretty one in the family. All the boys are going to be after her, I can tell you. And this is Selina, the baby of the family. She is so cute, and she says the funniest things. A little comedian." Then she turned to me and hesitated. "And this is Angela . . . she has other talents."

The woman's words hit me like a ton of bricks. Even young children can figure out that the world values brains, beauty, and humor. But what does it do with "other talents?" My childhood and teen years were spent in a disheartening search for what my "other talents" might be. And slowly, I'm finding them. I've got a sharp sense of humor, a good ear for words, a passion for literature, a fabulous memory, and . . . oh, what was that other thing I was going to mention? Never mind, you get the point. That's why stories like Bill Walsh's appeal to me. Bill turned around, found something he *was* good at, and made a success of it. And then he very magnanimously gave back to those who had helped him see his potential. Bill Walsh is an overcomer because he didn't let anyone corrupt his confidence. **Overcomers believe in themselves.** They know they have something worthwhile to contribute to society. They know their two cents' worth is really worth it. They know that no one else can take their place in life.

On July 6, 1942, Michael Sylvester Stallone came into the world. Baby Stallone, born in a charity ward, suffered permanent damage to his facial nerves when an impatient doctor used forceps to pull him out. For the rest of his life, his speech would be colored by a minor slur. The boy also suffered from rickets as a child. He was the target of all sorts of abuse from neighborhood roughnecks. Michael's dad also beat him.

But rather than retaliating at the world or becoming a roughneck himself, Michael took his considerable anger and channeled it into bodybuilding, and later into acting. It was a good decision. His acting and screenplays have made Sylvester Stallone one of the richest and most successful people in Hollywood.

Where would Sylvester Stallone be today if he had not had such confidence in himself? And where does such rock-steady confidence come from?

Who Loves You?

The most basic, ground-level starting point for believing in yourself comes from knowing that you are loved.

In Maya Angelou's book *Wouldn't Take Nothing For My Journey Now*, she tells of a lesson she learned many years ago from her voice teacher, Frederick Wilkerson. Wilkerson asked Angelou to read a passage from the book *Lessons in Truth*. This passage ended with the simple line, "God loves me."

Each time, Maya read it through in just the manner she thought Wilkerson wanted, but each time he insisted that she read it again. Finally, on the seventh read-through, Maya Angelou began to cry. She realized the truth of what she was reading. As she said, "I knew that if God loved me, then I could do wonderful things, I could try great things, learn anything, achieve anything."

Who we are, our whole approach to life, is profoundly shaped by those who love us. Do you agree? Then listen to these words from the Bible, Romans 8: 35, 37-39: *"Who shall separate us from the love of Christ? Shall tribulation, or distress, or persecution, or famine, or nakedness, or peril, or sword? . . . No, in all these things we are more than conquerors through Him who loved us. For I am sure that neither death, nor life, nor angels, nor principalities, nor things present, nor things to come, nor powers, nor height, nor depth, nor anything else in all creation, will be able to separate us from the love of God in Christ Jesus our Lord."* Overcomers know they are loved, and they believe themselves worthy of that love.

Overcomers also know they are worthy of reaching their highest, God-given potential. You are worthy of success. What is the use in settling for less than the best?

Once you actually see your potential, you are forced to make a choice: to ignore that potential and fail to live up to it, or to strive to fulfill it. And make no mistake about it: passivity in the face of your potential is just as much a choice as is the active decision to pursue your potential to its highest fulfillment.

George Lopez drifted aimlessly through high school, spending his idle moments picking fights with local gang leaders. Then a history professor, Donald Haydu, began encouraging George to set some goals and plan for the future. He realized that his deepest passion was to be a doctor. He had no money, no academic background, and no support from his family, but George Lopez had a dream. He began arriving on campus at 6 a.m. to study. In class, he asked detailed questions, never letting a matter drop until he understood it completely. Each night found him in the library. And George never doubted that vision of himself as a successful doctor.

Today, George Lopez runs a thriving medical practice, with many other doctors working under him. The medical company he started holds six patents on devices or procedures used to save lives and advance the cause of medicine.

Another wonderful story. Wonderful, but rare. So many young people are without goals, without purpose, without identity. They have no clue as to their potential, the unique gifts and abilities God gave them. They can only see who they were in the past, or who they are in the present. How radically would it change their lives if they could see who they're capable of becoming in the future? Wait a minute! How radically would it change YOUR life if YOU could see YOUR real potential? (*Thought you were going to let that one slide, didn't you?*)

God knows who you were in the past and who you are in the present. But He can also see who you're capable of becoming in the future. Satan is the accuser, the one who is constantly reminding us of our past. God is in the change business, and the person God wants to change is you. And that's exciting. We have much to look forward to, 'cause God isn't finished with us yet.

Hiding In The Wine Press

Pull out your Bible and turn to Judges 6: 11-16. In this story, an angel of the Lord appears to a young Israelite named Gideon, as Gideon is threshing wheat in a wine press. If we had lived back in those days, we would have known from this first sentence what kind of person Gideon was. He was a cautious person. A timid person. In the South, where I'm from, the less-charitable folk among us might call Gideon "yellow-bellied." Why? Because, wheat is always threshed up on a hilltop, where the wind can blow through it and carry away the lighter-weight chaff and leave the heavier wheat kernel behind. But Gideon was threshing wheat in a wine press, a deep pit where the grape-stompin' traditionally took place. So why was Gideon threshing wheat—a traditional hilltop activity—down in the wine press? He was hiding, that's why.

You see, the Israelites were currently being persecuted by a tribe of nasties called the Midianites. Their favorite tactic of war was to swoop down on the Israelite tribes and steal or destroy their crops. So let's not be too hard on poor, shaking-in-his-shoes Gideon. I'd be hiding from the Midianites, too.

Let's take a little reflection break here. Can you identify with Gideon? Do you have your own personal wine press, a place where you go to hide from certain situations? I remember my wine press well. As a child, I was painfully shy, and nowhere was my shyness more crippling than at school dances. I would arrive at the dance full of breathless expectation, convinced that *this time* I would enjoy myself. But soon, my self-consciousness and nervousness would take over, and I would hide out in the bathroom until the evening was over. Oh, how I cried with shame and frustration. Nobody likes to be in hiding.

But back to our story: An angel of the Lord appeared to Gideon as he was hiding and threshing wheat, and this angel greeted him with the words, "The Lord is with you, you mighty man of valor." Say what? "The Lord is with you, you mighty man of valor"? Was this angel a few beans short of a burrito? Gideon must have thought so, because he replied along the lines of, "If God is with us, then what's with all the persecution from the Midianites? The Lord's dropped us like a bad habit." But the angel tells Gideon that <u>he</u> will be the one to deliver the Israelites from the hands of the Midianites. Gideon must have thought he got an angel-in-training that day. Can't you just see it? He probably started talking re-a-l-l-y s-l-o-w-l-y a-n-d d-i-s-t-i-n-c-t-l-y so the angel would be sure to understand him. He said, "Behold, my clan is the weakest in Manasseh (the town where he lived), and I am the least in my family." Don't you feel for the poor boy? But the angel of the Lord assured Gideon that the Lord *would* be with him, and he *would*, by golly, whup those Midianites, and that's all there was to it. And that's exactly what happened.

Now, why in the world did we just go through all that? Because of the moral of the story: God could see in Gideon things that Gideon couldn't see in himself. All Gideon could see was who he had been in the past and who he was in the present. But God saw who Gideon could and would be in the future. He knew the potential He had placed in our poor, cowardly protagonist. And God stood ready to equip Gideon *just as soon as Gideon accepted his calling*. There's the catch. We have to be ready to accept our calling from God. We have to be ready to use the potential God gave us. Then God will equip us for the task.

But how do people learn to see their God-given potential? Here's a story we can all learn from:

Charles' parents had an unhappy marriage. After their divorce, his father lost touch with the family. Charles, his mother, and his brother were plunged into poverty. Charles' mother turned to drink. She became verbally and physically abusive toward her sons. School officials, other family members, and the police refused to help.

I've just described for you the true life story of Charles J. Givens, the creator of the world's most successful financial planning company, the Charles J. Givens Organization. Givens is a multimillionaire and the author of best-selling business and personal improvement books. He is happily married, with a close family.

How did he do it? It would have been easy, given his background, for Charles Givens to spend his life hiding in the wine press. But somehow, over the years, Charles J. Givens realized that his fears and his low self-esteem stemmed from the messages he received in his childhood. Once he decided that the past wouldn't control him, he was able to set positive goals for his future.

Les Brown is a top motivational speaker and businessman. Les has the drive to excel in anything he tries. This ambition, to a certain extent, springs from the discouragement he faced early in life.

One day, young Les was clowning around at school. The principal, outraged by his antics, began screaming at Les, calling him retarded and a troublemaker. That day, Les and a handful of other students were removed from the fifth-grade and put back into the fourth grade. He was labeled a special-education student, and called slow and dumb. Throughout his high-school years he was consigned to the lower level classes. Instead of destroying his self-esteem, the principal's cruel label drove Les to work harder and achieve more throughout his life. He showed the world that no one could give him a negative label and get away with it.

Don't you love it? Don't you just *love* it? The overcomer does not let others define him. He (or she) realizes that labels are for boxes, not human beings.

Elton Richardson didn't learn to walk until age two due to a nutritional deficiency that left her legs weak and bowed. As an adult, Elton shuffled everywhere she went. She was tired and in constant pain. When the doctor confined Elton to bed, she escaped her boredom by eating large quantities of junk food.

Finally, Elton decided to take control of her health. She began reading nutrition books and cleaning up her diet. A radio report about senior marathon runners inspired Elton to begin walking regularly. At age 48, she took up race-walking. Since then, Elton Richardson has set 28 American records and four world records in her sport. She garnered eight national championship titles in 1994. At the 1996 World Championships, she earned three gold medals. She was voted 1994 USATF Female Master Racewalker of the Year, and she has been nominated to the USATF Masters Hall of Fame. How did she do it? How did an overweight, physically hampered woman decide one day that she would change her life? Elton Richardson decided to reach her potential. She decided that her own life was worth an investment of time and effort. She realized that she had unexplored horizons of greatness within her. Don't you want to discover the same thing?

Success For Dummies

Every overcomer has this hard lesson to learn: you must trust in your potential, even when others don't believe in you. Elias Howe's obsession with ideas and inventions, as opposed to more practical ventures, often left his family in a precarious financial situation. To make ends meet, Mrs. Howe took in the neighbors' sewing. Watching his wife bent over her painstaking work must have fueled some of Howe's desire to invent a sewing machine.

It took years of frustration and failure before Elias Howe was able to create a workable sewing machine. In the meantime, Howe's beloved wife died, and he lost all his earthly possessions. Other inventors claimed that they had designed the first sewing machine. But after an expensive court battle, Elias Howe secured his rights to the patent. Honors and money began pouring in. Remembering his own days of hardship, Howe often used his riches compassionately to help others in need. Unlike some inventors, Elias Howe tasted the sweet fruits of his labor before he died.

It can't be easy to hang on to your vision when everyone else is blind to it. Imagine the ache of having a dream that no one else believes in. That's why it is so vitally important that you believe in yourself. If you're sure of your potential, and you're committed to your passion, then don't let anyone discourage you. Learn from the story of John Kilcullen of IDG Books.

John was rising in the ranks of Bantam Doubleday Dell Publishing Group, but he wasn't satisfied with his job. John had a vision of a new line of books for the computer illiterate. When Bantam showed no interest in his idea, he quit and joined International Data Group, Inc.

IDG was willing to back John on his idea of super-simple computer guides for the common person, but they didn't like his proposed title, *DOS for Dummies*. For a while, it looked like the critics were right. His first few books failed miserably. But John dug in and worked harder. He believed his idea would catch on eventually.

John Kilcullen is now president and CEO of IDG Books Worldwide, Inc. In four years, his division has expanded to 200 different books, translated into more than 28 languages. Twenty-five million "... *for Dummies*" books have been sold so far.

John Kilcullen's story is inspiring. He overcame the naysayers. He persevered when others thought he was wasting his time. The human spirit is a wondrous thing. If the heroine of this next story hadn't held on to her vision and believed in herself, millions of people may have suffered needlessly. Her tenacity shaped history.

In 1910, an epidemic of poliomyelitis struck the Western world. Doctors didn't realize that their best treatment methods, which involved straightening and binding the spastic limbs, contributed to the devastating nerve damage.

Against all popular medical wisdom, a young nurse from a small town in Australia began treating symptoms of poliomyelitis with hot compresses and massage. It worked! Muscle spasms disappeared and mobility returned.

Unfortunately, the medical establishment in Australia refused to believe that Nurse Elizabeth Kenny had come up with an effective treatment. So Nurse Kenny traveled throughout the U.S. and Europe, sharing her methods there. By 1950, Elizabeth Kenny's methods for treating polio became standard practice worldwide. Before her death in 1952, she was recognized by the American Congress of Physiotherapy with its Distinguished Service Gold Key, the first woman to ever be awarded this high honor.

Never does an individual feel more alone than when he or she is holding fast to a vision that others cannot see. It would be tempting, in the face of such opposition, to lose sight of one's uniqueness. To blend in. But the overcomer is not afraid to stand alone—to excel in spite of others' designs against him.

The famed sculptor, Michelangelo, was regarded jealously by other artists of his time. At one point, Michelangelo was hired by Julius II to design and build a magnificent tomb. But two other artists, Raphael and Bramante, convinced Julius to re-assign Michelangelo to a lesser job, that of painting the ceiling of a local church. Not only was this a demotion of sorts, but it forced the sculptor to work in a medium he was not used to.

It took four years of backbreaking work to finish the painting, but it was worth it. For the ceiling of the Sistine Chapel contains one of the greatest artistic masterpieces of all time.

Do you trust that God has placed within you unique talents and abilities? Do you believe in yourself enough to ignore the criticism and push on anyway? Then you will be an overcomer, too.

Overcomers' Secrets:

1. Believe in yourself.
2. Know that you are worthy of reaching your highest potential.
3. Trust in your potential, even when others don't believe in you.

3

BUILD YOUR OWN FAN CLUB:
Surround Yourself with Encouragers

Louis Gonzales, Ph.D. is an educational consultant and the director of Center for Safe Schools and Communities. He is a man who values education. But Louis wasn't always like that. He grew up in a neighborhood where street-smarts were all that mattered. The best way to survive was to join a gang.

One day, Louis was goofing off with his gang friends when a teacher, Mrs. Olson, confronted him. She forcefully escorted him to her Speech and Debate class and made him sit there and listen. Louis realized that the skills he used every day for fast-talking and goofing around could be used in Speech and Debate to win an argument. He loved it! The more he excelled in school, the less he hung out with the gang. Today, Louis is actively involved in the field of education because one teacher took the time to encourage him.

Think back to times in your life when someone has encouraged you. Would you have learned the very basics of life—playing patty cake, tying your shoes, writing your name—if there had not been someone there to clap for you? I hope that when you learned to ride a bicycle, memorize your multiplication tables, or walk the stage for your high-school diploma there was someone there cheering you on. Someone who said, "You can do it! I know you can." Have you ever taken the time to thank God for that person?

When I entered middle school, I was one big bundle of anxieties, awkwardness, and insecurity. As I mentioned earlier in the book, I was the dumb one in my family, so school was not a place where I got my ego stroked. My teachers liked to remind me that my brilliant older sisters had done well in their classes. Why didn't I?

But it was different in Mr. Bush's class. Mr. Bush was an English teacher, and he was new to the school. He'd never had my older sisters in class. And he thought I was smart. I remember the day he took me out in the hallway, looked me straight in the eye, and told me that he thought I was a talented writer. I could swear I heard the "Hallelujah Chorus" echoing through those corridors! Was this the "other talent" that woman at church had mentioned years ago? Mr. Bush liked the stories I wrote, and he wanted to submit them to a national children's magazine. I never did get published in that magazine, but I didn't care. Someone outside my family had said I was talented. His words of encouragement helped to shape my identity and ambitions for years to come. **People who see and encourage the best in you are a gift from God.**

Kay Cole James has served as the secretary of health and human services for the state of Virginia, and as the associate director for the Office of National Drug Policy under former President George Bush. At her interview before joining the ONDP, a representative brought up the question of abortion. Ms. James answered with a question: "What would you say to a black woman who was barely twenty years old, with only a menial job and two children if she came to you and told you she was pregnant and the father had run off?" The representative recommended an

34

abortion. Then Ms. James explained that the example was from her own life. Kay Cole James had been that third child. Her mother struggled to raise three children by herself, but she gave her children a sense of identity, and taught them that they could triumph over circumstances.

In the first two chapters, we discussed what individuals can do to overcome their circumstances. But lest we start to think that success is a solitary pursuit, we must remind ourselves that no one achieves anything in life without a little bit of help from others. The great poet John Donne rightfully noted that, "No man is an island." **Overcomers aren't ashamed to look for people who will serve as their fan club, people who are gee-whiz, unabashedly enthusiastic about them.** God has placed us here to encourage one another.

Bette Midler seems the picture of brash confidence on stage. Yet it is a hard-fought confidence, earned in the face of discouragement and adversity. She was raised in poverty. One of her brothers was retarded. Her sister died in a car wreck. Midler's father had no interest in her career, but Bette had two things working in her favor: an immense amount of talent, and a mother who believed in her.

Ruth Midler encouraged her daughter in every way possible. She had to sneak out of the house to see Bette's movies or else her ill-natured husband would give her a hard time. Yet she did what she had to do to instill confidence in Bette. As Midler says, "My mother thought I could do no wrong."

One of the newest and most intriguing developments in the field of psychology is the study of resilience. Resilience denotes the ability to rebound from hardship, and a long-term study of 700 children from Hawaii is giving researchers insight into why some children overcome rough beginnings to create happy lives for themselves. The Hawaiian children, all born in 1955, came from a variety of backgrounds. Many came from poor or abusive families. Statistically, they were at high risk for adult dysfunction.

But the researchers discovered that most of these high-risk kids grew into stable, highly functioning adults.

Different psychologists explain this result in different ways. Some isolate certain personality traits that lead to resiliency, like insight and independence. Others point to the importance of people skills. Many resilient kids have an uncanny ability to find sources of support outside their families. They build a network of teachers, coaches, pastors, or other caring adults who give them the encouragement and guidance they need.

And sometimes encouragement can come from the strangest places. When Diane Hanny decided, at age 43, to get her college degree, only one obstacle stood between her and success: math class. Diane had avoided math most of her life, ever since her eighth-grade teacher, Mrs. Jamison, convinced her she was no good in the subject. Mrs. Jamison's snide comments squelched Diane's confidence in herself. Fortunately, Diane's college math professor, Mrs. Nash, was so encouraging and helpful that she began making A's in the course. She eventually graduated from college with honors. But here's the kicker: Mrs. Nash and Mrs. Jamison were one and the same person. Back when Mrs. Jamison was teaching eighth-grade math, she had been a very unhappy woman. In the years since, she had changed. Instead of a discourager, Mrs. Nash was now an encourager, someone who tried to empower her students and bring out their best qualities.

Diane Hanny's fears and self-doubt were caused by a woman who said, "No, you can't do it." And those same fears and self-doubt were forever healed by that same woman saying, "Yes, you can." So many of us are trapped by self-doubts, fears, or external circumstances until someone tells us, "I believe in you. You can overcome this. You are capable of more." And if we hear those words enough, we start to conform our self-image to the image others have of us.

Seeing People As Jesus Sees Them

A woman and her grandmother—a very forgiving and religious soul—were sitting on their porch discussing a member of the family.

"He's just no good," the young woman said. "He's completely untrustworthy, not to mention lazy."

"Yes, he's bad," the grandmother said as she settled into her rocker, "but Jesus loves him."

"I'm not so sure of that," the younger woman protested.

"Oh, yes," assured the elderly lady. "Jesus loves him." She rocked and thought for a few minutes before adding, "Of course, Jesus doesn't know him like we do . . ."

Are there people out there who know all about you, and still see something worthwhile in you? Then they are a gift from God. **Trust that others can see in you qualities that you cannot see in yourself.**

My parents live in Knoxville, Tennessee—home of the basketball dynasty known as the Tennessee Lady Vols, coached by the female version of God (at least as far as Knoxville people are concerned), Pat Head Summitt. The Lady Vols are amazing to watch. They have taken basketball to new heights. Part of their success is due to Coach Summitt's commitment to discipline and detail. She demands excellence from her players. Some players are harder to reach than others.

As a freshman basketball player at the University of Tennessee, Carla McGhee didn't attend practices if she didn't feel like it. She skipped the practice drills that didn't interest her. She lived according to her own rules. But then, in 1987, McGhee was in a devastating car accident. Doctors weren't sure she'd ever walk again. Teammates, fans, and even opponents filled McGhee's hospital room with gifts and cards. Their kind gestures humbled her. As she said, "In my own eyes, I had become nothing, and yet all of these people still loved me . . . that will just move you beyond belief."

After a year of intensive therapy, Carla McGhee was back on the court. Not only did she play better than ever, but she also became the team encourager. And in 1996, Carla was chosen as a member of the U.S. women's Olympic basketball team. Carla McGhee's teammates saw past her arrogant attitude to the precious person she really is. They loved her in spite of her pride. And that love changed her. It gave her the power to overcome her injuries and return to basketball as a true team player.

Some people do take a little longer to get with the program. And some people have scars that make it difficult for them to change their perspective.

In 1977, Bill Fero's aunt approached him about housing a family of Vietnamese refugees. It seemed like the perfect arrangement. A veteran of the Vietnam War, Bill had lost both legs to a booby trap mine. He could use the help. Aunt Rose had no idea that Bill harbored a deep hatred for the Vietnamese.

When the Vietnamese family arrived, Bill demanded they do all the hardest work around the farm. He hoped to make them suffer. But the family returned Bill's anger with kindness. When this family moved on, Bill allowed another Vietnamese family to move in. They, too, responded to Bill's bitterness with love. So did the next family. Finally, Bill Fero was worn down by the love of these Vietnamese families. His anger and hatred melted away.

Since 1979, Bill Fero's farmhouse has been a temporary home to more than forty Vietnamese families.

Bill Fero had been trapped by his hatred until the love and care of a few refugee families transformed him from a bitter man with no hope to a loving man with an energizing purpose. Those families looked past his anger and cruelty to see a valuable human being. They saw the worst in him and loved him anyway. Once Bill Fero saw himself through the eyes of the Vietnamese families, he was never the same again.

It is amazing how simple acts of kindness can change a life. Something as humble as a hug can transform another human being.

Dave's mother was an alcoholic. She beat and burned Dave, and forced him to live in their cold, dark garage. When one of Dave's teachers tried to intervene, Dave's mother punished him by changing his name to "It." She never called him anything else. The only comfort little Dave had in his life was the kindness of his schoolteachers.

A few members of the school staff finally convinced authorities to step in and remove Dave from his home. That day, the whole staff of Dave's school lined up to give him a hug.
Twenty years later, Dave Pelzer returned to Thomas Edison Elementary School to thank those teachers for saving him. As a motivational speaker, Dave now spreads his message of inspiration to thousands of people. In 1994, he was honored with the Outstanding Young Person of the World Award.

Can you imagine overcoming years of abuse and neglect to create a healthy, successful life for yourself? How did Dave Pelzer ever do it? We don't know all of Dave Pelzer's formula for overcoming, but we can rest assured that it all started with the simple act of encouragement.

What Can't Be Taken From You?

In 1986, Greg LeMond became the first American cyclist to win the prestigious Tour de France bicycle race. It looked like a great start to an illustrious sporting career. But on April 20, 1987, his dreams came to a screeching halt. While out turkey hunting with relatives, Greg was accidentally shot in the chest. Bullet fragments spread throughout his body and lodged in one lung. Greg wasn't sure he'd ever race again, until he heard his doctor comment to reporters, "There's absolutely nothing permanently wrong with Greg."

Those simple words restored Greg LeMond's spirits. He committed himself to a re-conditioning program. Others in the cycling world may have thought he was finished. But since 1987, Greg LeMond has won two more Tour de France races.

One simple comment from his doctor changed Greg LeMond's perspective. One simple comment reinvigorated him. He overcame his injuries to win the Tour de France again.

Think of some comments others have made to you or about you that affected how you saw yourself. It's important to ask ourselves, why is our self-image based so much on others' thoughts and opinions? Think about it: in childhood, we develop definitions of who we are.

I distinctly remember the day I allowed someone to define me. I was in fourth grade, and the teacher had just assigned the students to work in small groups. I was placed in a group with Peanut Beeler (his real name was Troy), the cutest boy in fourth grade. I pulled my chair over next to his, blushing furiously the whole time because I was in such close proximity to *the* cutest boy I'd ever seen. He leaned back in his chair, smirked, and said, "Did you know you're the ugliest girl in the school?" Don't ask me why, but I believed him. And I died a shy little girl's death. Only formerly shy little girls know the slow, heart-crumbling-into-a-thousand-pieces, big-lump-stuck-in-the-back-of-your-throat, hot-tears-of-shame sensations involved in a shy little girl's death. At that very moment, I allowed Peanut Beeler to define me, to change the way I thought about myself. Why would I even care what someone named *Peanut* thought? But that's how insidiously we allow others' opinions of us to become the truth about us.

Think about your friends, your kids, your spouse. Can't you see positive qualities in them that they can't see? Don't you think they can see positive qualities in you that you've never noticed? What's the source of this innate blindness to our own potential? Whatever it is, it's past time to confront it. That's the only way to overcome old, limiting definitions of ourselves.

Dat and his sister Dung (pronounced Young) were outcasts in their society from the day of their birth. Amerasians, children of mixed birth, face all manner of discrimination in Saigon. In addition, the children were orphans, desperately poor, and Dat was blind. Brother and sister survived by begging in the streets.

Dat's one joy in life was listening to American music on the radio. He often drummed along with the beat. A blind music teacher, Mr. Truong, was so impressed by Dat's drumming that he gave him free music lessons and money to live on. Mr. Truong got Dat interested in the classical guitar, and helped him get into a college music program in the U.S.

In 1994, Dat Nguyen won the Southern California American String Teachers Association competition. Today, Dat has turned to composing music. He donates part of his income to help Vietnamese refugees in the Philippines. Who knows how many other children out there have the same potential as Dat Nguyen? What will happen to that potential if we never discover and encourage it? What if stagnant potential began to stink, just as stagnant water does? We would be forced to confront all the greatness in our societies and in ourselves that is going to waste.

During the Second World War, Corrie ten Boom was imprisoned in a Nazi concentration camp. After Allied troops liberated the camps, many of the survivors were sent to refugee camps until they could be sorted out. At one refugee camp, Corrie met an elderly woman who had lost her will to live. The woman had been a music teacher and concert pianist at a prestigious conservatory before the war. She had lost everything, or so she thought. Corrie found an old, battered piano and convinced the woman to try it out. Her face glowed as she played Bach's "Chromatic Phantasy," an incredibly intricate piece. Corrie pointed out that the woman had not lost everything. She had saved something precious.

"And what was that?" the woman asked.

"Your music," Corrie replied. "For that which is in your heart can never be taken from you."

And that's the case with our potential, too. That which is in your heart can never be taken from you. But it can wither away from neglect. It can suffocate from lack of hope. It may never come to fruition without some encouraging words to nourish it.

Tough Love

Sometimes encouragement is disguised as tough love. We may chafe at it at first. We may not want to hear it. I can recall many times in my life when the most helpful words a person has spoken to me have also been the most hurtful words. But don't we all love an encourager? No, not really. Because those who encourage us challenge us to change. And change is frightening. It's an invitation to failure . . . or success. So we don't necessarily appreciate those who encourage us. Deep down, we're worried they could be wrong. But sometimes, we're even more worried by the prospect that they could be right.

In the 1960s Patty Perrin and her family lived in Afghanistan while her husband served in the Peace Corps. Patti was miserable in Afghanistan. She didn't know the language and she didn't have a purpose. She became isolated, and began turning to alcohol for comfort. And then Margaret moved in.

> "The nature of rain is the same, but it makes thorns grow in the marshes and flowers in the garden." —Arab saying

Margaret was a 14-year-old whose parents were also Peace Corps volunteers. Their remote area of assignment had no schools for older children, so Margaret came to live in the larger city of Kabul, with the Perrin family. While Patty had become passive and helpless, Margaret was active and driven. She was a go-getter and a risk-taker. Right away, Margaret confronted Patty about her drinking. So Patty gave it up. Although she could be a major pest, Margaret got Patty interested in life again. After a year, Margaret moved out. By then, Patty was actively involved in her community.

All encouragement, even the "tough love" type we resist, is a gift from God. Overcomers know the value of surrounding themselves with encouragers, people who see and encourage the best in them. If we let it, others' encouragement will eventually penetrate our thick skulls. And then our old, negative self-image, the definitions that we allow to hold us back and inhibit our potential, has to change too. And that leads us to the next stage in becoming an overcomer.

Overcomers' Secrets:

1. Look for people who will serve as your fan club.
2. Trust that others see in you qualities that you cannot see in yourself.
3. Sometimes encouragement is disguised as tough love.

4

QUESTION YOUR LIMITS: Who Says You Can't . . . ?

Most of us have heard the Zen-type question: how old would you be if you didn't know how old you are? It's pretty revolutionary if you think about it. It opens our minds to the possibility that "acting your age" is a social construct, not a foregone conclusion. What if we went through our lives with no preconceived notions about any certain stage in life? Teenagers wouldn't know they were supposed to be alienated and conformist. Senior citizens wouldn't know they were supposed to be cautious or conservative. It's a spine-tingling idea.

Now what if we flipped this question around: **who would you be if no one had ever told you there were limits to whom you could be? What would you be doing if no one had ever told you that there were limits to what you can do?** Would you be a different person than you are now? There are many people in this world who have found abundant success and happiness from overcoming the limits others placed on them. Let's begin with a woman who was born in 1867, the child of former slaves.

Sarah Breedlove's parents were sharecroppers who worked on a cotton farm. The institution of sharecropping was similar to slavery in that it still left the sharecroppers poor and dependent on the land owner. Sarah's parents left her an orphan at the age of seven, so she moved in with her older sister. Little Sarah had very little chance for an education because they needed her help on the farm. After suffering years of abuse from her sister's cruel husband, Sarah escaped by marrying at fourteen and moving away.

Tragedy entered Sarah's life again when a racist mob lynched her husband. The young widow had to figure out some way to support herself and her two-year-old daughter, Lelia. She worked long, hard days doing laundry for others. The reward for her hard work was that Lelia was able to attend school full time. Sarah was determined to give her child a better life.

One day, Sarah noticed that her hair was falling out. Many black women suffered from this problem because of the harsh measures they used to straighten their hair, to make it more like "white" hair. In a dream one night, a black man appeared to Sarah and gave her a recipe for a hair tonic that would regrow her hair. She ordered all the ingredients, some of which only came from Africa, and applied the tonic to her scalp. Soon her hair was growing back in abundance.

Sarah began marketing her new hair tonic, and soon earned a following of satisfied customers. She married again, to a man named C.J. Walker. Mr. Walker was a newspaperman, and he knew a little about advertising and mail-order businesses. With his help, Sarah's hair tonic business grew. However, business disagreements drove the two apart, and they divorced. For advertising purposes, Sarah changed her name to Madame C.J. Walker, and she began developing new products to add to her line. Her products sold like wildfire, and Madame Walker and Lelia began traveling the country advertising their products and training women in hair care and beauty. Soon Madame Walker was meeting and working alongside some of the early black activists and educators in this country, such as Ida Wells Barnett and Mary McLeod Bethune. Associations with these great women inspired Madame Walker to train black women for business. She set up a sales-training program for black women, and soon had scores of women working in her company. She also gave away large amounts of money to black charities. Once the business was an astounding success, Madame Walker began taking some time to educate herself. She devoured books on all sorts of subjects. She made up for all those lost years when work in the cotton fields kept her from an education. Her hard work and dedication brought her success undreamed of in those days, especially for a black person and a woman. Madame C.J. Walker became America's first female millionaire.

In that time and in that place, Sarah Breedlove wasn't supposed to run a successful business. It went against everything that society said was possible for black people and for women. So how did she overcome society's limits on her life? We can identify some of the steps on her road to success. She had a passion—making and selling her hair care products. She had a plan—setting up sales training programs for black women to market her products. She had personal mentors who encouraged her, like Ida Wells Barnett and Mary McLeod Bethune. But before she could take advantage of any of these things, Sarah Breedlove needed the ability to reject society's burdensome limits on her potential. She did that, and so can you.

So the next step on the road to success is this: **overcomers ascertain where their real limits are**. Are they mental? Physical? Emotional? Spiritual? Social? If you're going to have limits on your life or on your potential, at least be honest about what those limits actually are. The biggest prison in the world is the one we construct in our own brains. It's time to set yourself free.

You Gave Me A Mountain . . .

In 1789, Francois Huber, a Swiss naturalist, invented "the first movable-frame beehive," a marvel of science and engineering that sprung from Huber's intensive study of the habits of honeybees. Huber's research was so thorough that it still serves as the basis of modern research into honeybees. His work would be remarkable on its own, but one fact makes it even more extraordinary: Francois Huber was nearly blind.

Francois' wife, Marie, and his servant, Francois Burnens, aided him in his experiments and kept meticulous records of his work. With their help, Huber's genius had no disability to constrain it. His vital research, made possible through the devotion of his loving wife and servant, has had a great influence on our understanding of the natural world.

Obstacles come in many forms. Sarah Breedlove faced obstacles like poverty, racism, and abuse. Francois Huber faced a physical obstacle—blindness. Would it surprise you to know that some of the highest achievers started out in life with strikes against them?

In a study of high achievers (i.e. Nobel Prize winners), psychologist Mihaly Csikszentmihalyi of the University of Chicago, discovered that many were sickly children. This early hardship seemed to result in extra energy and strength in adulthood.

Dr. Csikszentmihalyi has come to the conclusion that being able to face adversity with a positive attitude creates in people a certain kind of self-assurance. Rather than wallowing in self-pity or passivity, these people learned to take charge of their life, focus their energies, and achieve great things.

Fanny J. Crosby (1820-1915), one of America's best and most prolific writers of Christian hymns, lived in darkness all her life. A doctor's mistake resulted in Fanny losing her eyesight in infancy. But she didn't let her disability keep her from living a full life. She taught at a school for the blind, married a musician, and wrote more than 2,000 hymns, among them "Sweet Hour of Prayer" and "To God Be the Glory." Who is to say what is or is not a handicap? Would you presume to tell someone like Fanny Crosby that she was missing out on life? Only the individual himself or herself can define what is or is not a handicap. We decide on our own limits.

In his early years, Winston Churchill struggled with two speech impediments, a stutter and a lisp. He never attended college. He fainted from fear during his first public speech, yet he became one of the world's great orators.

At one time in his life, Thomas Edison worked in a railroad yard. One day, he accidentally started a small fire in a freight car. The furious train conductor boxed him on the ears and threw him off the train. The blow to his ears left Edison partially deaf. Instead of wallowing in self-pity, however, he put his disability to good use. No longer distracted by the clutter of noise around him, he focused on his experiments. At his death, he held more than fourteen hundred patents.

A song from the early sixties is in the form of a prayer. The refrain, repeated time and again, goes, "It isn't a hill any longer; you gave me a mountain this time." Do you feel like you've been given a mountain to climb? The Bible says we can move mountains, if we believe. What is an obstacle? What is a handicap? Maybe those mountains are only hills after all. Maybe climbing them will make us even stronger and lead to greater accomplishments later. Resolve today to become a believer—and watch those mountains crumble.

Who Told You, You Can't Fly?

The end of childhood is the day we no longer believe we can fly. One day we wake up and realize that our bodies have built-in limits, that they can't automatically keep up with our imaginations. After collecting a few years' worth of bumps and bruises, the wise child realizes that some dreams are better left inside her head, not acted out. But accepting this reality often means sacrificing the daredevil confidence that marks a normal, chaotic childhood.

That's why I stand a little in awe of movie stunt people. They hurl their bodies into mortal danger with seeming disregard for the consequences. One special stuntman, R. David Smith, is the founder of Stunts-Ability, a program that encourages and instructs people with disabilities on how to get into the stunt business.

Smith was born without a left forearm, and he knows the prejudice that disabled people face. Some of Smith's clients are dealing with new and unexpected disabilities, such as those from an amputated limb. Learning a new and exciting skill like stunt work is actually a part of the healing process. As Smith tells new clients, "You're going to feel better about yourself than before your accident. I'm living proof." R. David Smith may have certain limits on his life, but they are not physical ones. Where are your limitations? Wherever you say they are.

When Dan Lawrence was diagnosed at 42 years of age with a very rare throat cancer, he bravely joked to his doctor, "I guess I'll never be a disc jockey." His humor reflects a life spent overcoming tough times. A veteran of the Vietnam War, Dan had flown many shipments of Agent Orange, the defoliant that has since been classified as a serious toxin. Dan's vocal chords were removed, and a digital voice synthesizer was installed that allows him to communicate in a monotone, mechanical voice.

But the joke's on Dan these days. He is now a radio disc jockey at station KHUM in Ferndale, California, where his format of "oldies" music, spiced with political and social commentary, is a big hit.

In the midst of our cheering for these overcomers, do we ever stop to think, *"Wait a minute, that's not supposed to happen"*? Blind people aren't supposed to make major contributions to science. Disabled people aren't supposed to make careers out of throwing themselves into danger. People without vocal chords absolutely can NOT work as radio deejays. But the overcomer answers back, "WHO SAYS?"

The question bears repeating over and over again: **Where do we get the limits that are placed on us**? Where did you get the idea that you could never achieve certain things? Who told you that you can't fly? Well-meaning parents or teachers, siblings and friends. Maybe you got the idea from past failures or embarrassments. I can tell you one place you didn't learn those limits. You did not get them from God. He created your potential. You magnify God's glory when you use your talents to the best of your abilities.

On Falling Forward

Most of our limits are rooted in fear. Prejudices, fear of the unknown, fear of change, fear of success, fear of failure—we're just a bundle of heebie-jeebies, aren't we?

Julius Caesar was the greatest military leader of his time. There was a time when he set his sights on conquering Africa. When the Roman boats landed on the African coast, Caesar was the first to step ashore. To everyone's horror, he tripped and landed flat on the ground. This was an era when people's lives were ruled by superstition, and Caesar's soldiers took it as a bad omen that their leader had fallen.

But Caesar was a clever man, and he knew how to turn the men's superstitions to his advantage. As he lay there on the ground, he spread his arms out wide and announced, "Africa, I embrace you." It was a bold, triumphant announcement, and the soldiers greeted it with cheers. With one quick-witted remark, Caesar had restored his men's confidence in his leadership.

Sometimes a perfectly able-bodied person is handicapped by a self-imposed or socially-imposed limitation, like the superstitions of Caesar's men. These types of limits can be just as real as a physical handicap, and overcoming them usually requires a radical change in perspective.

September, 1944—a U.S. bomber plane flying over the Pacific is hit by enemy fire. The three airmen on board make a hasty parachute jump to safety. Only one of the three survives the terrifying ordeal. This lone survivor, George Bush, would distinguish himself in business and in politics, and become our country's 41st President. Yet fifty-three years after the terrible bail-out over the Pacific, former President George Bush decided that he needed to tackle that parachute jump again. He wasn't looking for glory or publicity; he simply wanted to face the memories and emotions of this wartime incident. So, at the age of 72, George Bush hired a plane to fly him out over the Arizona desert, where he made a successful jump. Now, after all those years, he could put that part of his past to rest.

It reminds me of a statue I heard about in England. It is said that the English sport of rugby had its origins in a soccer match gone awry. According to the story, two English schools were engaged in a soccer match, when one excited player forgot the rules, grabbed the ball and ran with it toward the goal line.

The other players froze on the field, but the fans cheered wildly. And out of this incident came the hugely popular game of rugby. Visitors to England can see the statue that honors this young man's enthusiastic mistake. It is a statue of a boy, reaching down to grasp a ball. Part of the inscription reads: . . . *with a fine disregard for the rules . . . he picked up the ball and ran.*

That's what an overcomer does. With a "fine disregard" for their limits, they pick up the ball and run straight toward their goals.

To live outside one's limits requires a new perspective. Some people say, "Well, I'd have more impact on my life if my circumstances were different . . . If I weren't disabled . . . If my spouse were more supportive . . . If we were out of debt . . . If I could just get a lucky break . . ." Overcomers know that perspective is more important than circumstances. Eric Fromm wrote that, "Man is a product of circumstances, but the circumstances are also his product." Any circumstance can be turned to an advantage if we are determined to do so.

The citizens of Angels Camp, California, take pride in living in Calaveras County, the same county Mark Twain wrote about in his famous short story, "The Celebrated Jumping Frog of Calaveras County." In fact, they hold a frog-jumping contest at their annual Calaveras County Fair and Jumping Frog Jubilee.

One recent winner of the Jumping Frog Jubilee was aptly named Three Legs Are Better Than None. The three-legged frog was found in a canal and entered in the race, where his 20' 11" jump beat out all the other able-bodied frogs for first prize.

Three Legs' owner, Brian Cummings, believes that his frog lost one leg to a predator, and that the injury, rather than hampering the frog, may have inspired Three Legs to build up strength in his remaining legs.

Are you and I at least as smart as a frog? If life robs us of one leg, one skill, one opportunity—can't we strengthen what's remaining? If we must fall, can't we make certain that we fall forward? The perspective of an overcomer will conquer any circumstance.

Go Out and Make a Miracle

In *Chocolate for a Woman's Soul* by Kay Allenbaugh, Ursula Bacon shares how her family was forced by Nazi persecution to flee their country and settle in Shanghai, China before World War II. The Jews in Shanghai were forced to live in dirty, crowded ghettos. There were few jobs available, and most families struggled to survive.

These circumstances would be enough to scar any child for good, but Ursula kept a cheerful perspective with the help of a neighbor, Mrs. Rosa Goldberg. Every day, Mrs. Goldberg greeted Ursula with a smile and this piece of advice, "Well, darlink, Mrs. Goldberg will have to tell you again. . . . Go out and make a miracle today. God's busy, he can't do it all." These words gave Ursula that little boost of hope, that essential change in perspective she needed to make it through another day.

Whether you or I agree with Mrs. Goldberg's advice doesn't matter so much. The fact that she was able to give hope to a child living in desperate circumstances—that is golden.

Mrs. Goldberg knew that nothing is accomplished by sitting around feeling sorry for ourselves. After fear, despair and self-pity are the two most limiting emotions we can feel. They cause us to draw inward and nurse our wounds, rather than look outward and challenge our circumstances. And, as Morris Mandel says, "When we indulge in self-pity, we rob the poor and the suffering of that which is theirs by right and waste it on ourselves, to whom it does more harm than good." Good point! Nothing is more debilitating than despair and self-pity.

Georgia Griffith works as a systems operator and manager for seven different online forums for the CompuServe network. Every day Georgia moderates a wide variety of discussions on countless topics, and answers tricky technology questions that are sent her way. This would make for a full and challenging day of work for anybody, but it is slightly more impressive when you realize that Georgia Griffith is both blind and deaf.

Georgia was born blind, but she did not let her handicap keep her from graduating college or developing into an accomplished musician. But then, Georgia began to go deaf too. In 1981, a group of Georgia's friends bought her a specially-adapted computer, and she turned her remarkable intellect and drive toward mastering it. Her achievements have garnered her an online chat with Vice President Al Gore, and the Great Communicator Award, presented by Gen. Colin Powell.

Georgia could have easily given up, but through sheer determination she succeeded where other people would have failed.

In his book *The World's Greatest Comebacks*, Robert A. Schuller tells stories of ordinary people who don't let life's hardships keep them down. One such man is Mel Borchardt, a member of Schuller's congregation.

The date was July, 1986, and Mel, an accomplished pianist, was tickling the ivories when the left side of his body went numb. He had suffered a stroke. As the paramedics attended to him, Mel reached out his good right hand and began playing the piano again. A paramedic complimented him on his playing. Mel replied, "Wait till you hear me with both hands." He was getting into fighting spirit already.

Slowly, and with much effort, Mel regained strength and mobility in his left side. In spite of all his therapy and hard work, Mel's left hand just wouldn't cooperate. But he wouldn't give up his passion for the piano. Mel played with his right hand and programmed a synthesizer to round out the sound that would have been provided by his left hand. News of Mel's talent and perseverance spread, and soon Mel was being hired to play for all sorts of events and civic organizations. So once again, in his later years, after suffering a stroke, Mel Borchardt was a professional musician.

I love the story that journalist Nick Clooney tells of his uncles, William, George, and Chick. William and George fought in World

War II. But Chick, who had lost an eye to childhood meningitis and a finger to infection, couldn't pay the armed forces to take him. He spent the war years working as a recruitment officer.

Not long after the brothers' discharge, William, Chick, and George visited a local bar to swap war stories. Bar patrons listened respectfully as William and George shared harrowing tales of combat. Then it was Chick's turn. He popped out his glass eye and rubbed its shiny surface. He wrapped his maimed hand around his beer mug, and remarked, "I suppose you could say there are some things about war that a man will never be able to forget."

Chick's comment earned the Clooney brothers free drinks for the rest of the week.

No self-pity. No sulking. No despair. Ursula Bacon, Georgia Griffith, Mel Borchardt and Chick Clooney found themselves in difficult circumstances. They suffered from physical limitations that could have caused them to turn inward and withdraw from life. But they chose instead to do their best within their own limitations. They are too busy enjoying life to have a pity party. They took Mrs. Goldberg's advice. They went out and made a miracle. When we read stories like this, we have a choice: we can envy the overcomers for their great attitudes and achievements, we can make excuses for our own bad attitudes and lack of achievement, or we can change. That's it. There is no prize behind door #1 or door #2. But if we choose door #3, we just might open it to find ourselves as we could be, ourselves as we've always dreamed of being. If that's not a prize, I don't know what is.

I Thank God For My Handicaps . . .

Before we overdose on a *rah-rah, life-is-a-bowl-of-cherries* attitude, let's remind ourselves that each of these people had to face some dark times in order to develop a positive perspective. It's not easy to re-define ourselves. It doesn't come naturally. It requires a resolve, a firm decision to oppose both our negative inner voice as well as what others may say or think. **Overcomers know it takes courage to question our limits.** It takes courage to face down others' prejudices. Take the case of Bernard—a story of true courage, of overcoming a definition that had been placed on him his entire life.

In 1972, journalist Geraldo Rivera did a shocking exposé on Willowbrook, a care facility for retarded persons. Geraldo's sources included a few doctors and nurses within Willowbrook and one brave patient, Bernard Carabello.

Born with severe cerebral palsy, Bernard had been placed in Willowbrook at the age of five. None of the doctors at the overcrowded facility seemed to notice or care that Bernard wasn't retarded. He spent sixteen years of his life locked away in an institution.

Willowbrook was overcrowded and filthy, and patients were frequently neglected or abused. After

> In one of the delightful Uncle Remus tales, wise old Brer Fox tells Brer Rabbit that you can't run away from trouble—there "ain't no place" that far.

Geraldo's exposé, the federal government began pushing through legislation to create higher national standards for nursing homes and in-patient care facilities.

And what happened to Bernard after the exposé hit the airwaves? He got his own apartment, took speech therapy classes, and found work at a local charity foundation. Thousands of lives are better today because Bernard Carabello was willing to share his story.

What a waste it would have been if Helen Keller had not been delivered from the prison to which her disabilities seemed to have consigned her. Her remarkable story of achievement, in spite of being both blind and deaf, has inspired millions. After her teacher, Annie Sullivan, opened up the world of language and communication to her, Helen's hunger for learning never ended. She read widely, and wrote eloquently of her life. She graduated from the prestigious Radcliffe College with degrees in English and German. She gave popular lectures on important issues of the day, such as women's voting rights. She traveled extensively and befriended prominent people around the world, including President Eisenhower. In wartime, she visited military hospitals, encouraging those soldiers who had been wounded or disabled in battle. In her later years, Helen said, "I thank God for my handicaps, for through them, I have found myself, my work and my God."

Can we thank God for our limits? Winston Churchill's wife, attempting to console him after his 1945 defeat at the polls, suggested that this might prove a blessing in disguise. Churchill replied, "I am more conscious of the disguise than the blessing." That is where most of us are. And it is understandable. It takes a special kind of person to look a hardship in the face and say, "You will not defeat me!" The point is you and I can be that special kind of person. We can be overcomers.

Justice Louis Brandeis once advised his impatient daughter, "My dear, if you would only realize that life is hard, things would be so much easier for you." Life is hard, but God has given us the resources to overcome that reality. It is only when we face our limits and decide to challenge them that we can truly call ourselves overcomers.

Overcomers' Secrets:

1. Ascertain where your real limits are.
2. Most limits are rooted in fear.
3. It takes courage to question our limits.

5

DEVELOPING YOUR SKILLS: Turning Failure Into Ice Cream

The famous singer and songwriter Mel Tormè evidenced great talent at a young age. His satiny voice and boyish charm opened many doors for him in the show business world. As a teenager, he was chosen to audition for the part as a drummer in a Hollywood movie. Mel was already an accomplished drummer, but he was insecure about his acting ability. When he got to the audition, he became even more discouraged. He was auditioning against a very handsome, talented young man. Mel steeled himself for rejection. But then, they asked the handsome young man to play the drums. He was awful. He had no rhythm, no experience. Mel got the part.

Even in an image-conscious society like ours, true overcomers stand by this principle: **Skill wins out over lesser but more dazzling qualities**. Nothing can replace true competence. The world waits with open arms for that person who can get the job done right. And a truly skilled person is outstanding in many ways. The acquisition of skills requires discipline, concentration, hard work.

Karoly Takacs, a Hungarian marksman, had set his sights on entering the 1940 Olympics. He was acknowledged as the "European pistol champion of the decade," and an esteemed member of the Hungarian World Championship Pistol Shooting Team. But then, in 1938, the unthinkable happened: Karoly lost his shooting hand in a grenade accident while performing his military duties. Immediately after the accident, Karoly went into seclusion, and seemed to give up on life. But then he began practicing his target-shooting skills again, this time with his left hand. The global disruption of World War II caused a cancellation of the 1940 and 1944 Olympics, so Karoly had many years in which to practice, to hone his skill with a foreign hand. And when the 1948 Olympics came up, he was ready. Karoly Takacs won gold medals in the 1948 and 1952 Olympics while shooting with his left hand.

When Karoly Takacs lost his shooting hand in the grenade accident, the conventional wisdom would be that he had lost his skill too. But the grenade accident hadn't taken away his drive, his determination, his focus, his sense of discipline. Once these qualities are ingrained in a person's character, nothing can steal them away. In a world satisfied with mediocrity, they are like the cream that rises to the top.

Nicolo Paganini, a famous violinist of the nineteenth century, gave his most memorable performance with a broken violin. Paganini's concert before a packed Italian opera house was going splendidly. And then, one string on his violin snapped. Paganini played around it. A few moments passed and two more strings snapped. But Paganini, a true master of the instrument, was able to improvise the rest of the song beautifully on only one string.

There's a story of skill at its finest. Paganini's outstanding skills overcame the major inconvenience of a broken violin. That level of virtuosity has earned Paganini an esteemed place in the history of music.

Another person whose legendary skill earned her a place in history is Annie Oakley, the American markswoman. Adversity forced Oakley to develop her shooting talents early in life. Annie's father died when Annie was only four, leaving behind a large and impoverished family. Her widowed mother relied on little Annie to put food on the table. Not only did she hunt enough game to feed her own brothers and sisters, she sold the surplus at market and paid off her family's mortgage. Eventually, Annie would marry a fellow rifleman whom she had beat in a shooting contest. Her fame spread nationwide when Annie went on tour, demonstrating her remarkable skills for show.

Annie Oakley is a sterling example of someone who used her skills to overcome hardship in her life. Just like a forest fire burns off dead undergrowth and allows new trees to take root, adversity burns away complacency and replaces it with a fine determination to overcome one's circumstances.

Overcomers know that the easiest way to build a valuable skill is to start with what you know best.

Ben Cohen and Jerry Greenfield are the creators of the oh-so-sinful Ben & Jerry's Ice Cream, a gourmet brand known for its intense flavor and big chunks of ingredients. Their ice cream is a smash hit, taking in $150 million a year. But there is an interesting story behind their success.

Ben and Jerry went to school together, and they describe themselves as "nerds" and "uncool," never quite fitting in with any group. As adults, their professional lives were filled with failures. Finally, they decided to open an ice cream business together. But Ben suffers from a very weak sense of smell and taste. So he and Jerry made a game out of creating the most intense flavors possible. This way, the taste-impaired Ben could recognize them with his eyes closed. And that's how Ben & Jerry's got its start.

I know it's kind of sick to rejoice in another's disability, but aren't *you* glad that Ben Cohen has a weak sense of smell and taste? I know I am. Well, now that I've admitted that distasteful side of my character (pun intended), let me take it one reprehensible step further: I'm also grateful for this next guy's disability. Just bear with me on this one.

Back before dyslexia was a diagnosable condition, teachers thought that people like Stephen were dumb. Stephen flunked first and fourth grade. The teachers at his private school considered him so hopeless that they asked him to leave. Also, Stephen was a constant daydreamer. Later, when he flunked the tenth grade, and just barely graduated high school, everyone must have thought that Stephen's teachers were right. He just wasn't very smart.

But they changed their opinion a few years later, when Stephen put his daydreaming talents to work in the television industry. Stephen J. Cannell became one of the top creators, writers, and producers in all television history. Some of his shows include *The Rockford Files*, *The Commish*, *The A-Team*, *Baretta*, and *Hunter*. His production company produces some of the most popular shows on television, and his outstanding work has won him several Emmy Awards.

Ben and Jerry were ice-cream lovers. Stephen J. Cannell was a daydreamer. Who would have thought these qualities could be used to turn a profit, or improve others' lives? But these men started with what they knew best, and they developed their skills from that point. That simple formula has brought these men astounding success. So my apologies to Ben and Jerry and Mr. Cannell for getting pleasure out of your pain. But in my opinion, you gentlemen have been good stewards of your adversity. And that is the hallmark of the overcomer.

How Do You Spell Defeat?

Overcomers seize their opportunities where they can find them.

During the Civil War, Edmund McIlhenny and his family fled the advance of Union troops on their town in Louisiana. It would be two years before the McIlhennys would return home. Their sugar plantation and salt works had been destroyed. The family didn't know how they would make a living. As he inspected the grounds of their former estate, Edmund McIlhenny noticed something new growing in the garden: hot Mexican peppers. He began experimenting with the peppers, and eventually came up with a zesty new hot sauce. We know it as Tabasco sauce. Look in almost any grocery store in the nation and you'll find a bottle of McIlhenny's Tabasco sauce, still made by the McIlhenny family.

You can't keep a good man or woman down. Overcomers don't notice what they don't have; they take advantage of whatever they do have.

For 19 years, George Valassis worked in his uncle's advertising business. Then the uncle retired, and George's cousin took over. One of his first executive decisions was to fire George.

Shaken by the loss of job security, George decided to start his own business. Fortunately, his 19 years in the advertising trade had given him insight into what businesses need. Major companies had often encountered problems in trying to get coupons to their customers. So George began gathering coupons into booklets and placing those booklets in newspapers. It was the most convenient way to get the coupons directly to the customer. In fact, those coupon booklets you pull out of your Sunday newspaper are called "Valassis inserts," after George Valassis himself. George eventually sold his business for a major profit.

That's a story that should encourage us all. A little guy stepped on by insensitive corporate type makes a big success for himself in his own business! I'd bet that almost anyone who has ever lost his job has had that dream. But there is a vast difference between having a dream and having a dream come true. And that difference is spelled *d-e-t-e-r-m-i-*, oh, all right, you get the picture. Webster's defines *determination* as "the act or process of determining fixed purpose; resolution; adherence to a definite line of action."

Of the 800,000 or so Jews who passed through Treblinka, a brutal World War II concentration camp, there were only nine known survivors. One of those survivors was a young man named Manfred. All of Manfred's family, immediate and extended, died in the Holocaust. He was an orphan, completely alone in the world.

> If God sends us on stony paths, He provides strong shoes. — Corrie Ten Boom

At the age of 24, Manfred made his way to the United States. He began life in America with a new name, Fred Kort, and with one shiny nickel in his pocket. This was all the money he had in the world. Fred got a job, began taking night classes, married and started a family. With hard work and determination, he moved up in the business world, and eventually opened his own company, the Imperial Toy Corporation. Last year, Imperial registered sales of $100 million.

Say what? That's right, $100 million. With a starting capital of one measly nickel. And remember, he had no family or friends to rely on. He lost everyone in the war. After surviving a concentration camp, Fred Kort earned the right to sit in a corner the rest of his days and have a pity party. He earned the right to be a basket case. So what happened? Mr. Kort must have decided one day that he would overcome his circumstances, he would overcome his past, he would build a better life for himself no matter what that took. THAT is determination.

At age 12, Paul Gonzales was shot in the head by a gang member. This would just be the first of many brushes with trouble. At 15, he was arrested for a murder he didn't commit. Paul's life seemed to be heading for a literal and figurative dead end. But that's not what happened. Paul happened to have a real skill for boxing. A police officer noticed Paul's abilities and began training him. At first, Paul's gang friends were, shall we say, less than supportive. But when they realized how serious he was, they began nagging him to get his sleep and stay away from drugs and substances that would hurt his body. All that hard work paid off when Paul Gonzales won a gold medal in the 1984 Olympics as a light flyweight.

Overcomers have one trait that separates them from the rest of us: they don't know how to spell defeat. Each time they get knocked down, they get right back up again. They can't be stopped because they won't be stopped. And because they won't be stopped, they accomplish more than other people even dream of.

Out of The Dugout

Joseph Sorrentino is a juvenile court judge in Los Angeles County. Judges have great power over the lives of others, and so they must possess wisdom, a boundless knowledge of the law, and good character. Joseph accumulated a knowledge of the law in school, but he developed many of his other qualities on the street.

Joe started life in a rough neighborhood in Brooklyn. He dropped out of high school after his first year and joined a violent street gang. Then he enlisted in the Marines, only to be kicked out with a dishonorable discharge for fighting, among other things. Joe Sorrentino was only twenty years old, and already he had chosen a rough and desperate path for himself. He went back to his old street gang, the Condors. The leader of the Condors was Joe's hero. The day Joe had to go down to the police morgue and identify his hero's body was the day Joe Sorrentino's life changed forever.

Remembering the encouragement of an old high school teacher, Mrs. Lawson, Joe went to night school to get his high school degree. He got a day job plucking chickens. Next, Joe moved to Los Angeles and started classes at UCLA. He joined many campus clubs and organizations, and was voted the student body president. Instead of joining the job market after graduation, Joe re-enlisted in the Marines. He just couldn't live with the fact of his earlier dishonorable discharge. After serving his term, Joe received an honorable discharge from the Marines.

Next stop was Harvard law school, where some people looked down on the law school student with the tough-guy voice and manners. No problem. Joe concentrated on improving his speech and manner, and eventually won Harvard's forensics competition. The crowning victory at Harvard came when Joe was voted the class valedictorian.

Once Joseph Sorrentino had a goal, a fixed purpose, in mind he focused all his energies on reaching that goal. In a race for excellence, those people who run that extra mile will always come out as winners.

In 1965, Mack C. Gaston worked as an ensign on a Navy destroyer, the USS Buck. Lieutenant Marvin, the man in charge of Mack's training, informed him that part of his duty was to answer three questions each day about the Navy. Each wrong answer earned him extra work. That first day, Mack stood watch for 24 solid hours before he finally got his three questions right. But he began learning everything he could about the Navy to meet Lieutenant Marvin's challenge. One day, Mack discovered that he was the only ensign being put through this ordeal. He was also the ship's only black officer. Mack's anger only fueled his drive to succeed. Soon, he could answer any question Lieutenant Marvin asked. In six short months, Mack was promoted to Officer of the Deck. He went on to achieve the rank of rear admiral, and in 1992 he was named commander of the largest training base in the Navy.

Could you or I blame Admiral Gaston if he had let his anger become a negative force in his life? Once he realized that he was being discriminated against, he could have soured on the armed forces, or given up trying, or only done enough to get by, or tried to get re-assigned to a different officer. He would have been justified in doing any of these things. But he chose instead to use his anger as a tool of motivation. He honed his skills in such a way that those around him had no choice but to take notice.

The pages of history fairly burst with stories of those who used hard work and integrity to overcome racism and discrimination.

The year was 1856, and a little boy was born into slavery in West Virginia. He was named Booker T. Washington. After the war, Booker was freed from slavery. He spent his childhood working in the West Virginia salt mines. Many black parents in the community pooled their resources to hire an educated ex-soldier to teach reading to their children. Booker proved to be an excellent student.

At the age of sixteen, Booker T. Washington set out on a 500-mile journey, much of it on foot, to Hampton Institute, a high school for black students. He was determined to further his education. Once there, he asked a teacher for admission to the school. The head teacher instead told him to sweep and dust a classroom. Imagine the frustration and humiliation he must have felt. Shut out from so many opportunities, Booker had worked hard and traveled far in order to get there. And now they were telling him to clean a classroom. But without a word, he began cleaning that room. He dusted it four times and swept it three times. The impressed teacher admitted him right away.

> **After all, a smooth sea never made a successful sailor. — Herman Melville**

Booker T. Washington went on to become a great orator and leader in education. He taught at the Tuskegee Institute in Alabama, and made the fledgling school into "one of the world's leading centers of black education," according to the Encyclopedia Americana. He also established the National Negro Business League, to create greater opportunities for others.

Overcomers know that competence is the great equalizer. Highly-skilled people command respect. They are able to transcend social (color, gender, culture) and physical limitations to reach their highest potential. If you have the skills that somebody needs or wants, they will overlook your color, your gender, your ethnic background. They will have to put their prejudices on hold because they need you.

Golf champion Tiger Woods inherited a love of the game from his father, Earl Woods. But how did Earl Woods learn to love golf?

Many years ago, when Earl was a lieutenant colonel in the Army, another officer challenged him to a round of golf. Discrimination kept most African-Americans off the courses in those days, so Earl Woods had never played. The officer deliberately gave Earl bad advice. Even worse, the two men had bet money on the game. Afterwards, the officer took every opportunity to tell others of Earl's defeat.

For the next six weeks, Earl played golf obsessively. He analyzed every move, honing his skills in an amazingly short period of time. In a re-match round, Earl shaved eleven strokes off his score, beat the officer, and won back the money he had lost. In the process, he gained a new passion for the game of golf.

The primary reason people cheer their hearts out for Tiger Woods is his outstanding athletic skill. The secondary reason is they realize what a remarkable amount of discrimination people of color have faced in the sport of golf. When you watch Tiger Woods play, you can't help but reflect on the legacy behind the excellence.

In the Presidential elections a few years back, the colorful Governor from Texas, Ann Richards, accused George Bush of being born on third base and thinking he had hit a triple. Some of the most successful overcomers in our society were not born on third base. Due to the prejudices or inequities of our society, they were still in the dugout when the game started. But they gave their best. They acquired the skills they needed. And today they are overcomers in every sense of the word.

Seize The Day

Zig Ziglar, the super-successful salesman and motivational speaker, loves to remind people of what they can achieve if they will put forth the effort. He cites the story of Vince Robert as proof of this. Vince dropped out of school in the fifth grade. As an adult, he found a job driving taxis. Taxi drivers often experience lulls in their business, times when they have to sit and wait for a fare to come along. To pass the time, Vince bought a huge dictionary and began teaching himself new words every day.

As he mastered new words, Vince gained a new sense of confidence too. He began to invest his money and to make goals for his future. Today, Vince Robert is the proud owner of Eighteen Cab Car Company. On the side, he also works as a motivational speaker, telling others of his road to success.

Time waits for no man, as the saying goes. Regret is the by-product of wasted time. Steam serves no purpose unless it's harnessed and used to produce energy. In the same way, time not spent in pursuit of a purpose is time wasted. **One of the characteristics of overcomers is that they are wise stewards of their time**. They seize opportunities because they are forever vigilant, forever prepared.

Cal Ripken, shortstop for the Baltimore Orioles, is a man who doesn't waste opportunities. He is famous for his perfect attendance record. In thirteen years as a major leaguer, he never missed a game. He broke Lou Gehrig's record for most baseball games consecutively attended. When asked if he ever showed up on the field with many aches and pains, Ripken replied, "Yeah, just about every day."

What makes Cal Ripken an overcomer is that he still showed up, even when he hurt. He demanded the best from himself no matter how he felt. He knew that each new day is an opportunity to be his best.

Bill Toomey is another man who makes the most of every opportunity. He knows how to use his time wisely. Toomey, competing in the decathlon in the 1968 Olympic Games, spent some time researching his event thoroughly in order to give himself an edge. In his research, he learned that it has often rained during past decathlons. Silly coincidence, but still . . .

Most other athletes quit practicing when it started raining. Following his research, Bill Toomey forced himself to train in bad weather. And would you believe that at the 1968 Olympics in Mexico City, it rained during the decathlon? Bill Toomey won gold that day.

It takes extraordinary inconvenience to do what Cal Ripken or Billy Toomey did. They have to fight the perfectly human tendency toward inertia, toward mediocrity. Few things in life are as rare as the will to excel.

Bjarni Herjolfssen's name will never stand beside that of other great explorers in the annals of human history. Although his story unfolded approximately one thousand years ago, it still holds value for people today. Bjarni set sail for Greenland in search of his father. His ship veered off course in a storm, and Bjarni found himself approaching an unfamiliar island. It didn't look like Greenland, so Bjarni didn't stop. A second time Bjarni's ship sailed within sight of an unfamiliar land mass, and a second time he refused to go ashore. He was looking for Greenland, and that was that!

When Bjarni returned home, he was called before King Earl Eirik to tell about his trip. The king chastised Bjarni for passing up unknown lands. He had lost the opportunity to claim new land for his country. He had lost his chance at glory.

Don't pull another Bjarni, my friends. God has blessed you with an immeasurable reservoir of talent, potential, and strength. Don't bypass the opportunity to discover your potential, to conquer new terrain, just because it's unfamiliar to you. Accessing that potential will require investing in hard work and determination.

But at some point, we all have to decide if we want to be king of the hill or run of the mill. You don't have to be the same person tomorrow that you are today. Just as chance favors the prepared mind, God favors the skilled person. He will not let your efforts go to waste.

Overcomers' Secrets:

1. Skill wins out over more dazzling qualities.
2. Seize your opportunities where you can find them.
3. Competence is the great equalizer.
4. Be a wise steward of your time.

6

USE YOUR LIFE FOR SOMETHING MEANINGFUL:

No "Ig Nobel" Aims

Each year, the Massachusetts Institute of Technology and a magazine, the *Annals of Improbable Research*, bestow a prize on the scientific research or invention that is most ridiculous or of questionable value to society. It is called, appropriately enough, the Ig Nobel Prize. In years past, they have awarded the Ig Nobel to a French scientist who concluded that calcium buildup in eggshells was the result of cold fusion, and to a South Carolina engineer who calculated the odds of Mikhail Gorbachev being the Antichrist at more than eight billion to one. The inventors of blue Jell-O have also been honored with an Ig Nobel.

Many people spend their lives playing "trivial pursuit"—and I don't mean the board game. They spend their lives seeking that which can never satisfy. What do you work for every day? Success? When most of us think of success, we think in terms of huge paychecks and public acclaim. That's only natural. Our society reinforces this definition in our minds every day. Money is the measure of the man, at least here in the United States. But we all know that God has a different definition of success, one rooted in fulfilling His purposes.

Overcomers know that standards of success and failure change when you're talking about meaningful work. Big bucks and ego strokes lose their significance.

But where can we find a person who exemplifies both society's and God's definitions of success? Let's start with the anonymous Baltimore businessman who is sending young, black boys from rough inner-city neighborhoods to a boarding school in Africa.

The Baraka School, a boarding school for young men between the ages of 12 and 14, is located in a remote area of Kenya. There the boys get an education and a new way of life. The school is run by two married couples, one white and one black. Since most of the boys are from single-parent homes in predominantly black neighborhoods, these two couples provide for them a model of healthy marriages and interracial friendships. The boys learn discipline and study skills at the Baraka School. There is no TV. Instead, the boys' energies are used up on such pastimes as climbing nearby Mount Kenya. Through hard work and personalized attention, these boys return to the States with broadened horizons and an improved sense of self-esteem.

The funny thing about the world's definition of success is that it doesn't guarantee fulfillment. Success and fulfillment are two very different creatures. Watching out for your own interests may make you a success. Putting the common good ahead of your own agenda earns you fulfillment. When we come to the end of our day, or the end of our lives, what will be the end result of our work? **Overcomers make their work and their lives mean something**. The anonymous Baltimore businessman is using his time, talents, energy and resources to open up opportunities for dozens of young people who ordinarily receive little of society's bounty. In creating these opportunities, he is helping to overcome the poverty, racism, and hopelessness that often constrict these kids' lives.

In some underdeveloped African and Latin American countries, millions upon millions of people suffer from river blindness. The condition is caused by the bite of a small fly, and results in itchy rashes, huge swollen bumps on the body, and eventually, total blindness. A few years ago, a research scientist at Merck & Company, a pharmaceutical firm in New Jersey, discovered that a heart worm pill they manufactured called Mectizan could prevent river blindness in those who hadn't yet been bitten, or stop the progression of the disease in those already infected.

So Merck & Company teamed up with the Carter Center, the humanitarian organization founded by former President Jimmy Carter, to distribute Mectizan to *every* individual in danger of river blindness—for free. By 1995, they had treated more than 14 ½ million people worldwide, and more people are benefitting from the program every year.

We have two ways of judging the success or failure of a firm like Merck & Company: we can look at their stock prices and financial statements, or we can look at what they are doing to make the world around them a better place in which to live. I don't have a head for business; lock me in a room with Peter Lynch and Warren Buffet, and I still couldn't interpret a financial statement to save my life. All I know is, millions of people who were destined for blindness will now be able to see, all because a company halfway around the world from them cared.

Profiles in Courage

Overcomers know that living a meaningful life requires transcendence: the commitment to using your life for something beyond your own fulfillment.

Humorist Robert Orben writes, "The world now has so many problems that if Moses had come down from Mount Sinai today the two tablets he'd carry would be aspirin."

Who's going to argue with that? And some problems we face, like crime, pollution, government corruption, can be traced directly to self-centeredness, the mindset that says, "I'm going to get what I want, and to hell with how my actions affect other people." The irony comes from the fact that our self-centeredness hurts us just as much as it hurts other people. But isn't self-centeredness natural? If we don't watch out for our own best interests, who will? Maybe God? Hmmm . . .

In 1966, evangelist Billy Graham planned a series of revival meetings in the town of Americus, Georgia. Unfortunately, he was having no luck finding a local clergyman who would sponsor the meetings. The Graham organization, by committing itself to lead only integrated meetings, had made itself unwelcome in some parts of the South. No local leader wanted to risk the scorn, ostracism, and possible violence of his neighbors. Finally, a state senator from a neighboring town offered to sponsor the crusade. He knew that he might be throwing away his political career, but he believed in the aims of Billy Graham's organization, so he took that chance. Did his courageous actions destroy his political future? Fortunately, no. In only a few years, that principled young senator was elected governor of Georgia. And in 1977, Jimmy Carter was elected the 39th President of the United States.

Jimmy Carter risked putting his principles ahead of political popularity. His decision may have had a very different outcome. We could all be sitting here saying, "Jimmy who? Never heard of the fellow." But Jimmy Carter was willing to take that risk because the cause of integration was more important to him than his own career and reputation. When you value your principles more than you value your own life, then you can't help but live a meaningful life.

> **I believe I've been helped by the realization that life is a series of struggles. And there's nothing I or anyone else can do about that. In fact, I've come to relish the struggles. — Donald Trump**

Most of America knows of Senator John McCain through his war record. McCain enlisted in the Navy in the late '60s. On October 26, 1967, he was captured by North Vietnamese soldiers and imprisoned in a POW camp. For the next five-and-a-half years, they starved and tortured him repeatedly. His suffering was beyond description. But his courage went beyond belief. You see, McCain could have gotten out sooner. The North Vietnamese had made that offer, but one policy of war is that "prisoners return in the order they had arrived." The North Vietnamese weren't trying to be kind; they made the offer because they knew that if McCain went home earlier, it would demoralize the other imprisoned troops. Also, it would be a breach of military code, and, therefore, a breach of honor. McCain is descended from a long family military tradition, and he knew the consequences upon his honor and upon the other soldiers if he accepted the North Vietnamese' offer. So he refused, and spent years in utter and unimaginable suffering.

These days, the Republican Senator works hard for financial reform in politics. He attacks pork projects and excessive government perks. He favors limiting the lobbying power of retired members of government, and he insists on working across party lines. He is vigilant about building alliances with both Republicans and Democrats who share his ideas. All this has made McCain mighty unpopular with some Senators. Why would he put his neck on the political chopping block? The answer springs from his high principles, principles forged during a time of personal suffering.

How did John McCain overcome the bitterness and pain that he must have felt toward his captors? How does he overcome the scorn that some of his colleagues feel toward him? He has a higher principle to answer to, a transcending purpose that fuels his work. The question is not, how could he overcome all the evil inflicted on him? With that kind of motivation behind him, how could he not?

Why Do They Do It?

The ruthless war that tortures Rwanda has left thousands of people homeless, among them the *maibobos*, the abandoned children resulting from the war. Some are orphans; some are the result of war-time rapes, and so they are ostracized in their villages. The streets of Kigali, the Rwandan capital, are filled with children, mostly boys, because the girls are snatched up to work as live-in maids or sold into prostitution. These children would face a future without hope, were it not for those few who are determined to help. A priest from Argentina, Father Carlos, moved to Rwanda in 1982 and opened a mission to Kigali's street children. The members of the mission attempt to teach the children a trade and to offer them odd jobs so they might earn a dollar or two.

Doctors of the World has joined with a Rwandan organization called Rafiki to plan a large farm where street children can be housed and taught a trade. The Rwandan government is building housing for the children, and getting some of them back in school or in job training and literacy programs.

One of the more unique patrons of the children is an Irish musician named "Mama Una." Mama Una has set up a flock of tents where forty or more children sleep each night. She finds food for the children, works with government officials on the children's behalf, procures medicine when they're sick, and responds to whatever needs the orphaned children have.

What motivates people like Father Carlos and Mama Una? They chose to move to one of the most dangerous and desperate places on earth to minister to strangers. They have dedicated themselves to overcoming evil and indifference in the country of Rwanda. Where did they get the courage and compassion to tackle such a daunting task? When we are asking why evil exists in the world, let's not forget to ask why there are people willing to lay down their lives to see that the results of evil are contained and someday crushed.

Bud Ogle lives and ministers in a poor, crime-ridden neighborhood in Chicago. He is a member of Good News Partners, an organization that provides whole-life help to those in need in his neighborhood. Good News Partners builds low-cost housing, runs soup kitchens, teaches parenting and job skills, runs a day care, and provides drug and alcohol rehabilitation programs.

A couple of years ago, Bud Ogle was preparing for an outdoor Easter service in his neighborhood when a pusher walked up and offered to sell him drugs. Bud was devastated that his Easter preparations were interrupted by the presence of evil. But the following year, as Bud prepared for the Easter service, he came across George—a former drug addict—standing vigil on the sidewalk near his headquarters. Two weeks earlier, two young boys had been murdered on that spot. George was standing vigil all day, every day until Easter, as a way to remind the community of the boys' murder.

Farther down the same street, Bud ran into a group of women also standing vigil. They had decided to claim that street for Christ, to disrupt the business of the prostitutes and drug dealers who usually occupied that corner. These women maintained a very public vigil to let people know that good would drive out evil in that neighborhood. The only thing these people were doing was standing on street corners. What gave their work its power? They were standing for God's presence in the world. And just a few people taking a stand can make a difference.

Wanted: Risk Takers

Overcomers also know that living a meaningful life requires a willingness to take risks.
When the pastor asked, "Will those of you who are willing to do anything necessary to lead others to Christ please raise your hands?" nineteen-year-old Celecca Cutts hesitated for a moment. But she sincerely wanted to share her faith with others. So, overcoming her natural timidity, she raised her hand.

A few days later, Celecca was involved in a serious car accident. She survived, but passed in and out of a coma for many days. Celecca's mother never left her side. She prayed over her daughter day and night. In that same room was another desperate mother standing vigil over her ill daughter. When Celecca emerged from her coma a few days later, the mother and daughter had both come to Christ, convicted by Celecca's mother's witness.

Doesn't that give you pause? Maybe the two events—Celecca committing herself to doing "anything necessary" and her subsequent car accident—were entirely unrelated. But doesn't it call to mind the phrase, "Be careful what you wish for. You just might get it"? Aren't we sometimes afraid that God will call us out of our comfort zone to do His work? That's what keeps most of us from giving ourselves wholeheartedly to any kind of bold venture. Fear is a natural by-product of taking a risk. How do we overcome that fear? By having a principle or a purpose that overrides our fear.

During the battle of Fredericksburg in the Civil War, Confederate troops gained the upper hand. After two days of fighting, the fields were carpeted with dead and dying soldiers, most from the Union side.

One Confederate soldier, Sergeant Richard Kirkland, asked permission to take water to the suffering men. His superior officer couldn't believe his ears. Didn't Sergeant Kirkland realize that he would be shot as soon as he stepped out on the field? But he let him go.

At first, both sides held their fire out of sheer curiosity. As they watched Sergeant Kirkland offer a cool drink to dying enemy soldiers, cheers rang out from both sides of the field. Whenever Sergeant Kirkland returned to his side to get water, shots were fired. But all fighting ceased the moment he stepped back onto the field.

That day Sergeant Kirkland earned the nickname, "The Angel of Marye's Heights."

If you're striving for fame or fortune, obstacles seem to pop up everywhere, and fear of failure is magnified. But if your sole purpose is to work for the greater good, obstacles suddenly disappear. Failure is not even a consideration.

Morris Dees heads the Southern Poverty Law Center in Alabama. The Ku Klux Klan and other hate groups count him as their greatest enemy. How did Dees earn such an honor? He has carved a career out of prosecuting hate crimes and advancing the cause of civil rights throughout the South. He faces constant death threats and intimidation, but says: "All I know is, if I failed to represent somebody because of fear, I wouldn't want to practice law."

In his greatest case yet, Dees prosecuted a couple of Klansmen who had abducted and lynched a young black man, Michael Donald. In the middle of the trial, one of the Klansmen approached Michael's mother in tears and asked for her forgiveness. And Beulah Mae Donald replied, "Son . . . I've already forgiven you." Her incredible show of grace brought everyone in the courtroom to tears.

Really, that's a story about three types of overcoming. Morris Dees overcame fear and intimidation by focusing on his purpose, advancing the cause of civil rights. The Klansman overcame his own hatred and sin to repent and ask for forgiveness. And Mrs. Beulah Mae Donald overcame her grief and anger to forgive the young man who killed her son. It could only be God's intervention in these three people's lives that allowed the story to end that way.

As World War I decimated Europe, a British nurse, Edith Cavell, began secretly caring for injured British soldiers. Her clinic, part of the underground movement defying the Germans, nursed injured soldiers back to health and, if necessary, secured them safe passage out of the country. In October 1915, Nurse Cavell and many of her comrades were arrested by the German forces. She was sentenced to death. In a letter to her pastor, Edith wrote, "I know now that patriotism is not enough; I must have no hatred or bitterness towards anyone." After her death, the story of Edith Cavell's bravery and commitment spread throughout the U.S. and Europe, and the number of new enlistments skyrocketed in response. Though she was gone, her passion inspired many others to come after her and carry on the fight.

Not only did Nurse Cavell's actions help to overcome evil, her struggle to forgive her captors was a personal journey of overcoming. Bitterness would have been the natural response, completely justifiable in a human sense. Only the working of the Holy Spirit in her life would have made it possible to overcome this hatred.

Sail On

Overcomers also know that living a meaningful life requires perseverance. Overcomers become overcomers by holding on in the face of daunting circumstances.

Joaquin Miller was a popular poet of the late nineteenth century, known for verses celebrating the rugged pioneer life. One of Miller's most popular poems was inspired by Christopher Columbus' courageous voyage to the New World. Titled simply "Columbus," it echoes a phrase found daily in Columbus' diary of his journey. In spite of danger, exhaustion, failing hope on the part of his men, and stirrings of mutiny among the crew, each day Columbus started his diary entry with the words, "This day we sailed on." He and his men were approaching a great unknown, with no guarantee that they would ever make it safely, yet each day his diary entry read, "This day we sailed on." Even today, we can be inspired by a determination so strong that, in the face of possible failure, it still sailed on.

Where does the drive to "sail on," even in the face of adversity, come from? Our next few stories give us a clue.

One of the little-known explorers of the American West was a Black man named Estevanico Dorantez. Originally from Spain, Dorantez and his crew of men were shipwrecked on the coast of Florida, where most of the men died from exposure to the elements and the occasional Indian attack. Estevanico and three of his men were left to explore on their own. For eight years they forged their way west, making friends with many Indian tribes along the way.

Estevanico's talents as an explorer and a scout earned him the attention of Friar Marcos de Niza, a friar from Mexico City who had heard many stories of huge, wealthy cities farther out west. Friar Marcos hired Estevanico Dorantez to guide a group of men to this legendary land. A cross of twigs sent back to Friar Marcos would indicate whether or not the men had found the cities. A small cross would mean nothing, but a large cross would mean that they had discovered the great cities of wealth.

One day, to Friar Marcos' great delight, an Indian from Estevanico's crew came into the village bearing a large cross of twigs. Unfortunately, Estevanico would not be able to share the Friar's joy. He had been killed by suspicious Indians. But he had led his crew through rough terrain to new territory, the land that we know as New Mexico and Arizona.

Like Estevanico Dorantez, a person with a purpose can only look in one direction—ahead. Their own lives and reputations no longer matter as much as does their obligation to the common good.

Raisa Gorbachev, in her book *I Hope*, shares how much of Russia's history has been a history of pain and suffering. This adversity has affected the country and its people in unique ways. She writes, "The most important thing that my parents gave me was a capacity to share other people's needs and to enter into their grief, their pain: the quality of empathy . . . No, not a single generation lives in vain on this sinful earth."

Not a single generation lives in vain on this sinful earth. Each one of us is significant in the eyes of God. But our lives are not our own. We were created by God, and as our Creator, He has first say on all we do or are. For our lives to have any meaning, we must dedicate ourselves to God's work. That doesn't mean we all have to enter the ministry. God's work can be done in raising a family; donating your time, talents, or resources to a charity; working for peace and justice in your society; giving an honest day's work on the job. And maybe, facing down a rough personal storm in your life and deciding to sail on.

Scars to Stars

Edward Sheldon once wrote: "God will look you over, not for medals, diplomas, or degrees, but for scars." Carolyn McCarthy knows about scars. She is one woman who was inspired by her personal sorrow to work for the public good. On December 7, 1993, a disturbed man boarded a train on the Long Island Railroad and began randomly shooting the passengers. Nurse Carolyn McCarthy went numb when she learned that her husband, Dennis, had been killed, and her son, Kevin, severely injured. When Carolyn learned that her state's Congressman wanted to water down gun safety and anti-violence laws, she was outraged. But she was just a nurse, a mother, a housewife—what could she do to change the situation? Well, Carolyn McCarthy decided to run against her representative, and she won. She is now the Democratic representative for New York. In this new position, Carolyn continues to push for stronger anti-violence legislation. She credits her success in politics to the courage and perseverance of her son, Kevin, who has surpassed his doctors' prognosis.

If anyone in this world is known for their passion, it's mothers. The average mother would cut out her own heart before she would allow her loved ones to be hurt. And what if they are hurt? Then what does a mother do? If she is an overcomer, she takes that hurt and uses it to make life better for other people.

On August 16, 1991, Dianne Clements' thirteen-year-old son, Zachary, went to play at a friend's house, and never came home. Zachary was killed that day, the victim of a gun accident. As the two boys were playing around the house, Zachary's friend found his stepfather's loaded shotgun. While inspecting the gun, the boy accidentally shot Zachary in the chest.

The Clements family grieved deeply for young Zachary, but Dianne Clements turned her energies to something other than her grief. She began giving speeches about Zachary's death to various groups. She researched the issue of gun accidents, and out of that research she established an organization called Zero Accidental Killings, Texans for Gun Safety. Her group works to reform gun laws and educate the public about gun safety. Zero Accidental Killings convinced the Texas legislature to pass a statute that restricts access to guns for people under the age of eighteen. In the two years after the statute was passed, Houston experienced a 50% decline in accidental shooting incidents involving children and teens.

Another story of mothers who dedicate themselves to the greater good comes from Rio de Janeiro, Brazil. Like any big city, Rio faces devastating social problems, such as street gangs and escalating crime. Unfortunately, certain sectors of Brazilian society have chosen to combat these problems by killing off young teens. Throughout Brazil, police and vigilante groups murder teen gang members, even those just suspected of being in gangs. And, of course, war between rival gangs adds to the number of murdered children and teens each day. In Rio alone, around 600 children are killed each year. In the face of such daunting evil, there is a group of mothers who have committed themselves to redeeming Brazilian society.

They call themselves "Wake Up, Deborah," after the Jewish prophetess who attempted to provoke the Israelite people to demand freedom from their oppressors. Numbering around 40,000, these women commit themselves to daily prayer for their children and their country. They take as their watchwords Hannah's prayer from 1 Samuel: "O Lord Almighty, if you will only look upon your servant's misery . . . but give her a son, then I will give him to the Lord for all the days of his life." Like Hannah, these 40,000 mothers pray that their children will become followers of Christ, and that they will then serve as missionaries to their society and their world.

Women of every color, language, and social class have joined the "Wake Up, Deborah" movement. They meet monthly in area churches to pray, encourage one another, and share their stories. At

89

many of these meetings, children who have been prayed for come forward to repent of their rebellion and give their lives to the Lord. In a society marked by danger and hopelessness, these faithful women believe that their prayers can change their homes, their society, and the world.

God honors our efforts to do His work. Carolyn McCarthy, Dianne Clements, and the mothers of Rio moved from "Someone's got to do something about this," to "*I've* got to do something about this." Each of them must have entered into their work with trepidation. What were their qualifications for changing the world? Nothing, except that they cared enough to do it. And God saw that.

Passion gives you purpose. And having a purpose gives you power. Because even one person with a purpose can affect thousands, or millions, of lives for the better.

Changing the World

In 1890, Jane Addams, a young woman from an affluent family, bought an old house in the heart of a poor Chicago neighborhood, and opened it to the public. Anyone could walk in off the streets and find help at Hull House.

She began teaching poor women to read, opened a day-care for children of working mothers, and created a modern kindergarten for street children. She agitated for a law against child labor. She convinced local lawmakers to set up the first juvenile justice courts in the country, and inspired President Taft to form the Children's Bureau in Washington, to oversee the affairs of the nation's children. During World War I , Jane worked for the League of Nations. In 1931, Jane Addams was awarded the Nobel Peace Prize for her work on behalf of the children and her nation.

Your life and mine have been affected, at least indirectly, by the reforms Jane Addams worked for over sixty years ago. How could one woman's influence stretch that far? Because God was behind her work. He prospered her efforts to the point that our whole nation was changed. But can one woman's efforts affect the whole Western world? A Quaker woman by the name of Elizabeth Fry did just that.

In the year 1813, Elizabeth visited London's Newgate Prison. She was shocked by the conditions. Hundreds of female prisoners, along with their children, milled about in the filthy, dark rooms. There were no opportunities for education or reformation. The more hardened criminals exhibited vile and violent behavior.

Elizabeth returned to Newgate often, and in 1816, she joined with other Quaker women to establish the Association for the Improvement of the Female Prisoner in Newgate. The Association provided clean clothing, job training, and spiritual and moral instruction to each of the prisoners. Practices that we consider commonplace, like the separation of various classes of criminals, basic education and training for gainful employment, and female guards for female prisoners, were all innovations that these Quaker women began. Elizabeth spent the last years of her life traveling across Europe, advising other governments on the issue of prison reform.

Elizabeth Fry's reforms are still bearing fruit today. One person really can make a difference in the world. And we don't have to hold political office or have great wealth to make that difference. All we need is an extraordinary level of commitment.

In 1947, war between Moslems and Hindus split the Mideast region. But one spot in all of India was an oasis of peace—the city of Calcutta. Mahatma Gandhi lived in Calcutta and held nightly prayer meetings there. Somehow, he had brought together the Hindus and the Moslems of the city and created a nonviolent pact between them.

When the war came to Calcutta, Gandhi vowed to fast until peace came . . . or death. Everyone knew a fast could kill the weak, elderly man. But he would willingly sacrifice his life for the cause of peace. Many people, moved by his devotion, began to demonstrate in the street. Some gave up their weapons; others publicly asked for forgiveness. Soon, a new peace pact was signed: "We shall never allow communal strife in the city again and shall strive unto death to prevent it." Only then did an ailing Gandhi end his fast.

How could one person have such an effect on so many people? How could prayer meetings and fasts make a difference in the midst of hatred and bloodshed? The only rational explanation must be that God honored Gandhi's work, that He infused it with the power to change men's hearts and minds. God is on the side of overcomers; His presence is the most essential aspect of their struggle.

Overcomers' Secrets:

1. Standards of success and failure change when you're talking about meaningful work.
2. Living a meaningful life requires transcendence.
3. Living a meaningful life requires a willingness to take risks.
4. Living a meaningful life requires perseverance.

Celine Dion, the French-Canadian pop-singing sensation, grew up in a small town, one of fourteen children. Family is important to her. Celine's show business career began in her family, when she and her siblings traveled around singing for various functions. And now, the internationally famous singer has sold more than 40 million records.

But Celine's young life has been marred by tragedy. A few years ago, Celine's young niece, Karine, died of cystic fibrosis. In honor of her niece, Celine does benefit concerts and raises money for cystic fibrosis awareness. For her wedding to manager Rene Angelil, Celine asked that everyone skip the presents and instead donate money to the Cystic Fibrosis Foundation. They raised $200,000.

7

HAVE FAITH IN GOD'S PLANS FOR YOU: Getting Back on the Wheel

In Matthew 17: 20 Jesus says, *"For truly I say to you, if you have faith as a grain of mustard seed, you will say to this mountain, 'Move from here to there,' and it will move; and nothing will be impossible to you."* That's one of those verses that most Christians love to recite, but do we trust it enough to act on it? Well, a little church in the Smoky Mountains did just that.

No sooner had the church finished construction on its new sanctuary when they got a notice from the county building inspector that their parking lot didn't meet regulations. They couldn't re-open until they had expanded it. But there was a problem: the church had been built up against the side of a mountain. So the pastor called his people together and declared they would pray to God to move the mountain behind their church.

The next day, a local construction boss came by. His crew was building a shopping mall nearby, and they had run out of fill dirt. Would the church sell them a chunk of its mountain? The crew would pave over the bare spot. Graciously, the pastor agreed. That

Sunday the members of this little church came together to praise the God who answered their prayers.

Have you ever thought of yourself as a mountain-mover? Have you ever thought of God as a mountain-mover? This whole book has been about overcoming, about moving mountains of some kind—prejudice, abuse, poverty, fear, failure, hatred, disability—that stand in the way of maximizing our potential, serving God, or finding fulfilment. And what have been the tools of the overcomer?

> †*A passion that stirs one to action*
> †*A belief in one's potential*
> †*The encouragement of others*
> †*A questioning of one's limits*
> †*Deliberate improvement of one's skills*
> †*Committing one's life to meaningful pursuits*

Now we've come to the final element in the O+ Factor, the foundation that undergirds the overcomers' efforts: a faith in God. You might be thinking, *Now wait just a minute. You don't have proof that all the people in this book believe in God. Some of them might not even be on speaking terms with the Almighty.* And you'd be right about that. But I believe that God has placed within every human heart an overwhelming, unquenchable sense of hope, and it is this hope, this faith, that ultimately provides the power to overcome adversity. Without hope, what reason do we have to persevere?

Overcomers believe that even in the midst of trouble God has plans to prosper them. Time to consult Webster's again: *To prosper* means *to cause to succeed, to do well.* Jeremiah 29: 11 reads, *"For I know the plans I have for you, says the Lord, plans for welfare and not for evil, to give you a future and a hope."* That's prospering us.

Whether we realize it or not, hope fuels every action we take. If we were to lose all hope, we would lose all reason for living. And a faith in God provides hope for the believer, even in the most hopeless of situations.

These words were found penned on the wall of a prison cell in Europe: "I believe in love even when I don't feel it. I believe in God even when He is silent." There is faith, hope, and love all thrown in the mix.

When the emperor Valens threatened Eusebius with confiscation of all his goods, torture, banishment, or even death, the courageous Christian replied, "He needs not fear confiscation, who has nothing to lose; nor banishment, to whom heaven is his country; nor torments, when his body can be destroyed at one blow; nor death, which is the only way to set him at liberty from sin and sorrow."

Most of us trust in God's providence because we secretly think God's agenda is the same as our agenda. We think our future will, for the most part, just keep getting better and better. Could we, like Eusebius, keep the faith if our immediate future were guaranteed to be full of misery and pain?

When William Sangster was told he was dying of progressive muscular atrophy, he made four resolutions and faithfully kept them: 1) I will never complain; 2) I will keep the home bright; 3) I will count my blessings; 4) I will try to turn it to gain.

Don't waste your time feeling sorry for William Sangster. Instead, take pity on the rest of us poor souls who whine over bad hair days and long lines at the ATM. We've forgotten the fact that God can aid us even in the midst of our troubles. We've forgotten the Mountain-mover.

When We "Fall Off the Wheel"

In 1992, a tragic car accident left Kendra Seaman with a serious brain injury. Her closest friend also died in the accident. Kendra's rehabilitation has been slow and strenuous. In spite of her struggles, Kendra praises God for His faithfulness. As she says, "I look at it this way. I was a lump of clay being formed by God. Somehow, some way, I fell off the wheel. I'm not blaming Him for that. But I am praising God because He put me back on the wheel and is reforming me." And what a beautiful, faithful vessel God is forming out of this young woman.

Do you know what it's like to "fall off the wheel?" Can you see where God was sustaining you at that time? Overcomers cling to their faith because they know that no matter what trials they go through, God still has a future and a hope waiting for them.

When Sir Harry Lauder heard the news that his son had been killed, he said: "In a time like this there are three courses open to one: (1) He may give way to despair, sour on the world, and become a grouch. (2) He may endeavor to drown his sorrows in drink or by a life of waywardness and wickedness. (3) Or he may turn to God." Why turn to God? Because our hearts were made for the presence of God. The highest joy we can feel is the joy that comes from God. The sweetest comfort we can know is the comfort that God gives to the broken-hearted.

Luther Bridgers, a pastor from Kentucky, wrote a very popular old-time hymn that is still sung at revival meetings all over the South. The first stanza and chorus are a sweet statement of joy and faith:

There's within my heart a melody,
Jesus whispers sweet and low:
Fear not, I am with thee, peace be still
In all of life's ebb and flow.

Jesus, Jesus, Jesus,
Sweetest name I know.
Fills my every longing,
Keeps me singing as I go.

These words must have come back to haunt Luther Bridgers the day he learned that his wife and two daughters had been killed in a horrible house fire. At the funeral, a neighbor asked Bridgers about his hymn. Could he still have music in his soul after this?

Luther Bridgers stood in silence for a long time, then answered: "If I know my heart, the music is resounding deep in my soul just as melodiously this moment as it ever has in my life."

Our hearts were made to hold the music of God. His love, His peace, His hope make up the melody that sustains us in times of trouble.

Thank You for My Hurting

The apostle Paul wrote in the book of Romans, chapter 5 verses 3 through 5, *"More than that, we rejoice in our sufferings, knowing that suffering produces endurance, and endurance produces character, and character produces hope, and hope does not disappoint us, because God's love has been poured into our hearts through the Holy Spirit which has been given to us."*

Dr. John Truman of Massachusetts General Hospital in Boston tells of treating a two-year-old leukemia patient named David. Even though David had to endure all kinds of painful treatments, he never complained. David's mother had explained to him in the best way she could that these doctors and nurses had to hurt him in order to heal him. They were doing it because they loved him.

At age three, David faced one of the most painful procedures any person could face, a spinal tap. The boy struggled and cried throughout the ordeal. But when it was over, little David looked up through his tears and said, "Thank you, Dr. Tooman, for my hurting."

If we were to take a clear-eyed look back at painful times in our lives, then maybe we, too, could thank God for allowing us to hurt. Because it is during these times that our faith has grown, our character has been forged, and our relationship with Him has deepened.

When Pastor Orson Vila was imprisoned by Cuba's Communist government, he started a new church in the prison. The other inmates asked Vila if his sentence were a punishment from God. He replied that it was a sign of God's love for them because he had been sent to tell them about Jesus. "God is good to me. He knew what He was doing. I needed the rest in prison," Vila said after his release nine months later.

What kind of prison are you in right now? A prison of fear, apathy, bitterness, pain, confusion? Can you, like Pastor Vila, start a church there? Can you invite Christ to come in and take over that part of your life?

Even Pastors Can Learn About Faith

A few years back, Matthew Woodley—a pastor in Minnesota—decided to leave the ministry. Over the years, a negative attitude had taken hold in his heart. He was tired of difficult people. He was tired of fielding everyone's complaints. He was tired of living in a run-down parsonage that the church refused to fix. He was tired of the church's constant money problems. Pastor Woodley had lost his focus, and he wanted out.

Not long after this, the Woodley family went on vacation to Montana. Matthew spent a day in a local park, praying and reading his Bible. As he prayed, three dirty, ragged little children entered the park and sat down nearby. The oldest child took it upon herself to make introductions. Her name was Deanna, and she was twelve years old. The other two children were her half-sister, Kristy, 10 years old, and her half-brother, Mikey, six years old. Deanna proceeded to explain that they were each sired by different fathers, and that Mikey's father was so abusive that the children's mother was filing for a divorce from him. The mother had dropped the kids at the park so that she could go gambling at the local casino. With a touch of sadness, Deanna reported that ever since their mother had lost her job, the family had been living in a tent on the outskirts of town.

When Deanna learned that Matthew was a pastor, she asked, "Mister Pastor, can you tell me something? I've heard stories about Jesus walking around healing people and loving people. Why doesn't he do that anymore?"

Matthew began stumbling his way through a deep, theological explanation, but he knew it didn't make sense to the kids. It didn't even make sense to him. These three poor, abused, neglected children needed to know the real story. So he stopped in mid-sentence, and, fighting back tears, said, "Deanna, Kristy, Mikey, let me start over. Do you have any idea how much Jesus loves you right now?" And Matthew shared the story of Jesus' love with those three children in the park.

As you might have guessed, Matthew Woodley never left the ministry. That day in the park brought him face-to-face with the loving, compassionate God that he had forgotten. It reminded him that ministry wasn't about pleasing people, or having a big church, or preaching the perfect sermon. It was about sharing the message of God with hurting people who desperately need to know they are loved.

Jesus broke into Matthew Woodley's prison of apathy and hurt. He renewed his spirit and prospered him, even in the midst of Matthew's troubles. Maybe Matthew Woodley could turn his back on his calling, but he could never turn his back on his faith in Christ. God used three poor, neglected little children to remind Matthew that He was still in control. And that He still loved him.

That is the hope that comes from God, a hope that does not disappoint us even when we are hurting more than we could possibly imagine.

Taking the Person from the Burden

Overcoming in the face of adversity might not mean complete and total restoration or healing. It might mean a spiritual and emotional healing, a change in perspective.

A man took a speed-reading course. He says that the only benefit is that now, when he reads a paper, he knows the bad news 10 minutes sooner than everybody else.

A woman called her husband at his office and told him, "I've got good news and bad news about the new car." "What's the good news?" asked the man. And his wife replied, "The air bag works."

We all know the bad news. Our faith in God will not always protect us from tragedy. Think that's bad news? It gets worse: Suffering may come to us because we are standing up for our faith.

In February 1962, a Cuban pastor by the name of Noble Alexander preached a sermon to his congregation on the topic of original sin. It would be the last sermon Alexander would preach as a free man for the next 22 years. Immediately after the service, Noble Alexander was arrested by the Cuban special police and sent to prison. To justify his imprisonment, the government drew up a list of false accusations against him, such as coming to the aid of counter-revolutionaries, attempting to assassinate Fidel Castro, and distributing opium. In government legalese, any preacher of the Gospel was guilty of distributing "opium" to the public.

For the next 22 years, they would torture Noble Alexander many times. He was imprisoned with mentally ill and sociopathic criminals. His wife left him for an army captain. She raised Noble's son as a committed Communist. Yet through all this suffering, Noble never stopped preaching about Jesus. He was moved from prison to prison, in the hopes that this would dilute his influence. But everywhere Noble Alexander was imprisoned, he shared his faith. Everywhere he went, he made converts. Though his words brought hope to the inmates, they earned him greater punishment from the guards. The Communist government didn't understand why Noble wouldn't accept their simple offer: freedom, in exchange for giving up his faith. Little did they know that it was Noble's faith in God that made him free, even while his body was imprisoned.

Alexander's mother and sister emigrated to the United States, where they worked tirelessly to publicize his plight. Soon, they gained the support of various activists, politicians, and the Reverend Jesse Jackson. With Rev. Jackson's help, Noble Alexander was deported to the United States in 1984. Today, he pastors two churches in Massachusetts. He has married again. His ex-wife has returned to the faith and asked Noble's forgiveness. And the first sermon he preached as a free man after 22 years in prison? It was on the subject of original sin.

Noble Alexander overcame years of imprisonment, torture, and injustice because of his faith in God. That's one of the toughest aspects of our faith. The bad news is, God does not always save us from our circumstances. The worse news is, sometimes we may suffer because of serving Him. But there is good news. Martin Luther wrote, "The world assumes that peace comes only when a burden is taken away. If a man is poor, he thinks of becoming rich. If a dying man can escape death, he believes he will have peace."

Luther had a different view: "On the contrary," he said. "Christ often allows the burden to lay on us. Rather than taking the burden from the person, He takes the person from the burden."

That's the key. God can take the person from the burden. In his book *The Chicken that Won a Dogfight*, Ben Burton tells about the day he and his twin brother, Len, were out working in the fields. Suddenly, Len began dancing feverishly and screaming for help. Papa Burton snatched Len up and began shaking the stuffing out of him until something fell out of his pants. It was a harmless lizard. Len had suffered a good scare, nothing else. The father asked, "Are you all right?" Len replied, "Yes. It was painful, but it didn't hurt." We may still go through painful times, but they don't have to hurt. God can give peace to the troubled heart that no outside circumstances can ever crush. Even the worst news can be transformed by the knowledge that God is with us.

Unanswered Prayers

A few years back, *The New York Times* ran a story on David Rotherberg, a little boy whose father, in a fit of rage, set the child's bed on fire while he was sleeping. David suffered third-degree burns over 95 percent of his body. His treatments are exceedingly painful, and his doctors predict that he may have to suffer through as many as five thousand surgical procedures in his lifetime to correct the damage.

How does David deal with this? He doesn't focus on all he's lost, or on the pain he has suffered and will continue to suffer throughout his life. David chooses instead to concentrate on the positive side of life. As he said at age seven, "I am alive! I am alive! And I didn't miss out on living! That's wonderful enough for me."

David's story stirs up conflicting emotions. We can rage against the injustice of a child suffering. But we also stand in awe of one so young who copes with his problems so courageously and cheerfully. Truly, the human spirit is an amazing thing.

I wish I knew why innocent people sometimes suffer. I wish I knew why Heaven is sometimes silent at the times of our greatest need. But this I believe: Just because God doesn't always answer our prayers the way we want Him to doesn't mean he has forgotten us. God sees realities of which we are not even aware. Somehow, someday, we will see that all the time God was working to our good. In the meantime, our prayers can change our perspective toward our circumstances, even if those circumstances don't change. God can give us hope and purpose even in the face of tragedy.

Baseball player Lou Gehrig had a bright future still ahead of him in baseball when he contracted ALS, a degenerative disease of the nerves and muscles. On July 4, 1939, the Yankees held a "Gehrig Appreciation Day." In his farewell speech, Gehrig remarked, "I may have been given a bad break, but I have an awful lot to live for. With all this, I consider myself the luckiest man on the face of the earth."

Not long before his death, Lou called up a friend, sportswriter Bob Considine, with great news. Researchers were testing a new serum for ALS sufferers. Nine out of ten people in the test group showed improvement. Lou was enthusiastic . . . in spite of the fact that he was that tenth man. Even when he was losing, Lou Gehrig had the attitude of a winner.

How can someone find joy, comfort, or hope in the midst of suffering? I don't know. That's a secret God reserves for those who have gone through the trials. It's part of the marvelous mystery of His love for us. But those who have gone through trials know that even if God doesn't turn back the clock and restore the *status quo*, He will still heal and restore their spirits if they trust in Him.

Horatio G. Spafford, a Chicago lawyer, went bankrupt in 1873. Not long afterwards, he sent his wife and four daughters on a trip to France. Their boat sank, killing the four Spafford daughters. Horatio set out for France immediately to be with his distraught wife. As he sailed for Europe's shores, he composed a hymn expressing his faith in the midst of grief. Millions of believers find comfort in Spafford's song, "It Is Well With My Soul." The first stanza reads:

> When peace, like a river, attendeth my way,
> When sorrow like sea billows roll;
> Whatever my lot,
> Thou has taught me to say,
> "It is well, it is well with my soul."

Our own Savior chose the path to Calvary, not Easy Street. We will suffer in this lifetime, and sometimes our prayers for deliverance will not be answered, at least not in a way we can perceive. God will not always save us from our circumstances. But here's the good news: He will give us strength, hope, and comfort in the midst of those circumstances, if we will ask Him. He will give us a new perspective on our circumstances, a new insight into our lives.

Hitting Bottom

Sometimes, **overcoming requires first admitting that we are powerless to overcome on our own.**

Two men were walking along the edge of a steep cliff one night when one slipped and fell over. His companion crept to the edge. "Are you all right?" he shouted. "Yes," came the answer from below. "Are you hurt?" he shouted back down. "No," came the reply. "Well," shouted the surprised man from above, "how far did you fall?" "I don't know," came the voice from below. "I haven't hit the bottom yet."

Often, it takes hitting bottom before we can admit that we need God's help to overcome our troubles. We're stubborn enough that we must exhaust all our own resources first. Only then do we crawl back to God and ask for His guidance.

The citizens of Goshen, Indiana were stunned to learn that Tracey Bailey—captain of the wrestling team, member of the student council, good student, from the church-going Bailey family—had been one of the teens involved in the devastating vandalism attack on the local high school. He was sentenced to a five-year term in the juvenile offenders facility. Originally conceived as a lesser form of penitentiary, this facility now held hardened criminals, even murderers and rapists.

In prison, Tracey gave up being a tough guy and gave his life to Christ. After his release, he made restitution to the school he vandalized. He decided he would pay back society by becoming a role model for other confused young people. He would become a teacher. In April 1993, Tracey Bailey attended a special ceremony at the White House where the President awarded him the National Teacher of the Year honors. Tracey Bailey wasn't ready to call on God until he had hit bottom. It was then that he finally stopped relying on his own strength. And God was faithful to His promise. God gave Tracy a new life.

When You're Ready to End It All

The largest Christian congregation in the world, the Full Gospel Central Church, is located in Seoul, Korea. This congregation of 500,000 people is pastored by Dr. David (Paul) Cho. In 1984, Pastor Stan Toler and his wife, Linda, traveled to Korea with some friends in the hopes of meeting this devout pastor. While there, they witnessed 2,000 people a day coming to be baptized at Dr. Cho's church. They were amazed to learn that Dr. Cho's first congregation consisted of a small tent and five faithful worshipers. At times he became very discouraged. Dr. Cho admitted that in 1969 he went to the roof of the church's educational building and considered whether or not to jump to his death. But God saved Dr. Cho from his discouragement. As he says, "God came to my rescue. Just in the midst of my discouragement, He brought me peace and encouragement!"

At his lowest point, Dr. David Cho gave up in despair, only to discover that God was just waiting to take over and bless him. God honors our turning to Him, even if we feel like slugs at the time. In our shame, we cry out, "Lord, I'm so lost, I'm so broken. I give up." And it is exactly at this point that God says, "Then give it all to me. That's just what I'm here for."

If you've ever been so desperate that you saw deliverance in the barrel of a gun, then Harold's story is for you. Harold had discovered alcohol many years ago, when he needed to escape the painful memories of serving in World War I. Over the years, his addiction had destroyed his career and his family. Finally, regret and shame overcame him, and Harold decided to kill himself. But as he aimed the shotgun at his head, Harold began to pray. And God filled him with a peace and a joy like Harold had never known.

He swore off alcohol that day, and began restoring his family and developing his spiritual life. Did it do him some good? Ask his wife Eva, or his two loving daughters. Or ask his constituents. You see, Harold Hughes, once a miserable alcoholic, became the governor of Iowa, and was later elected to the United States Senate.

Tracey Bailey, Dr. Cho, and Harold Hughes all came from very different backgrounds. They all struggled with different problems. But they all came to the same solution: only by giving up control of their lives and giving themselves to God were they able to overcome their troubles.

But here's the million-dollar question: If the life of an overcomer is so fulfilling, so joyful, then why isn't everyone an overcomer? Why are despair, self-pity, failure, hopelessness, and bitterness still tramping around in this world . . . and in our hearts? Because overcoming is hard. It demands more from us than we think we're capable of giving.

"No, I could never forgive my parents for abusing me."

"No one in my family has ever gone to college? Why do I think I can?"

"The boss hasn't liked any ideas I've come up with on this project. Why stick my neck out again?"

"What's the use of living if I'll never walk again?"

"I always screw up at (fill in the blank). What makes me think I can get it right this time?"

In most cases, we're right. We don't have what it takes to overcome that Mt. Everest staring us in the face. At least, not under our own power. But what about God? Is anything impossible for God? Not according to the Bible. Check out Matthew 19: 26: *"But Jesus looked at them and said to them, 'With men this is impossible, but with God all things are possible.'"* And in Mark 9: 23b Jesus says, *"All things are possible to him who believes."* Believes what? Believes in the transcendent power of God at work in our world.

Not Ready for Use—Healing

Suffering can harden a heart, or it can soften it to the point that the sufferer develops a unique capacity for empathy and compassion. **Overcomers don't let their experience lie fallow. They share their compassion, wisdom, and insight with others in need.**

Bruce Larson tells of meeting a man who had lost his wife in an automobile accident. The man claimed that a sign in his local park expressed his situation perfectly. The park service marked newly seeded areas of grass with a sign that read, *"Not ready for use—healing."* In his grief, the man believed he was not ready for "use" by God.

But Bruce replied, "No way. That's not you. That's grass. When you are healed, if that ever takes place, you will be less ready for use. While you are still healing, you can reach out to those who are experiencing grief and loss like nobody else."

And that's true. In the words of Henri Nouwen, "Only the wounded heart can serve."

Dr. Samuel Shoemaker was treating an elderly woman who had broken her hip in a freak accident. The break was so severe that the woman never regained her mobility. In the hospital immediately after the accident, the woman was in horrible pain. As Dr. Shoemaker treated her injury, the woman smiled up at him and said, "Well, I wonder what God has for me to do here." She was already looking out for God's providence in her misfortune.

That's the essence of the overcoming attitude. A person of faith, rather than moaning about his or her circumstances, looks around and says, "I wonder how God will use me here." They remain open to God's leading, even when their life has taken a detour. And they are willing to share their experiences with others, so that others may find hope or courage in their journey.

After years of faithful service to God, the Reverend Henry Francis Lyte was nearing the end. His doctor told him that he would succumb to his illness in a matter of months. Many who have faced death, especially believers, have noted that it brings a greater clarity and purpose to one's days. That is why Rev. Lyte was so saddened to see the pettiness and anger that simmered in his congregation. No matter how much he tried to share a message of peace and love with the people of his town, they wouldn't let go of the slights and feuds that had separated them for so long.

One dreary Sunday, when Rev. Lyte's words met once again with unyielding stubbornness, he flipped through his Bible for comfort. He came across a passage: "Abide with us; for it is toward evening and the day is far spent." Reflecting on those words, he suddenly became inspired to write a hymn, a hymn that is loved by millions.

Abide with me; fast falls the eventide;
The darkness deepens; Lord, with me abide;
When other helpers fail, and comforts flee,
Help of the helpless, oh abide with me.

Hold then Thy cross before my closing eyes;
Shine through the gloom, and point me to the skies;
Heaven's morning breaks, and earth's vain shadows flee;
In life, in death, O Lord, abide with me.
(1st and last stanzas)

The writing of that hymn took less than an hour. Yet, during World War II, when the *R.M.S. Stella* sank and killed 105 men and women, one woman on deck began singing "Abide With Me," and soon all the others sang along as they courageously faced their death. And when the nurse Edith Cavell faced German firing squads, she whispered the hymn, "Abide With Me." Who knows how many people have been comforted through the years by this hymn penned by a despairing and dying pastor?

In the midst of his own suffering, Rev. Henry Francis Lyte composed a song that has eased the suffering of millions of people.

He didn't conclude that he was "Not ready for use—healing," and the world has been blessed through him.

Blessed Are the Peacemakers

It takes a mighty faith for us to find good in the midst of evil, to find hope in spite of our sorrow. **The ultimate act of overcoming involves taking an evil act and squeezing some good out of it.**

In January 1995, Tony Hicks, a 14-year-old runaway from a fragmented home, shot and killed Tariq Khamisa, a twenty-year-old college student and pizza deliveryman. Tony, in the company of several gang members, had planned only to rob Tariq. At the last minute, the other boys bullied Tony into killing Tariq instead. Not long after the murder, Tony Hicks' grandfather, Ples Felix, got in touch with Azim Khamisa, Tariq's father. Azim invited Ples to his home, and the two men talked over their mutual heartbreak.

Today, Azim Khamisa and Ples Felix tour the country together, visiting schools and presenting a message of nonviolence. They discuss the lure of gangs and peer pressure. And they tell the story of Tariq and Tony—one child dead and the other in prison. In the face of a culture of violence and hatred, these two men provide a powerful example of reconciliation and forgiveness. This is faith in its most perfect form: when it removes anger, bitterness, and hate in our hearts.

John and Cathy Polec of Philadelphia relied on their faith to help them respond in a similar situation. It was the evening of November 11, 1994. The Fox Chase neighborhood in Philadelphia was calm that evening as sixteen-year-old Eddie Polec, his younger brother, Billy, and a few friends headed to the local recreation center to have some fun. Meanwhile, trouble was stirring in the nearby neighborhood of Abington. A rumor had started that a Fox Chase boy had raped an Abington girl. A group of angry young men from Abington armed themselves with baseball bats and poles and drove into the Fox Chase neighborhood. When they spotted Eddie Polec and his friends, the Abington boys decided to make them the target of their anger. The boys, seeing the approaching mob, ran in all directions. They didn't realize that Eddie had not escaped. The mob cornered him on the steps of St. Cecile Catholic Church, where they beat and kicked him to death.

His murder devastated Eddie's family. In spite of their grief, they immediately called on all Eddie's friends to keep the peace, not to retaliate against the Abington youth. Eddie's parents, Kathy and John Polec, announced privately and publicly that violence was the wrong response to Eddie's death. To bolster this peace, the Polecs appeared at numerous prayer vigils and anti-violence rallies, and repeated their message of peace and forgiveness, not revenge.

In the course of the investigation, police discovered that the local 911 service had received about 30 calls that night concerning Eddie's attack, but rude or incompetent operators had mostly ignored them. Although the Polecs would have been justified in suing the city, they didn't. As Kathy Polec said, "I refuse to put a price tag on the life of my son. We don't want to walk away with the money, we want the system fixed." Because of their efforts, the 911 system in Philadelphia has been through extensive changes, and now all police cars in the city are outfitted with special communications equipment.

Today, the Polecs still support rallies against violence, and everywhere they go they reinforce the message of no revenge, no retaliation. The police and many others believe this was the one thing that held their community together in the wake of Eddie's death. In 1996, hundreds of kids turned out at St. Cecile's Catholic Church for a memorial service for Eddie Polec. On the church grounds where Eddie was killed, they planted a cross upon which is carved the words, "Blessed are the peacemakers." How wondrous is the comfort and strength that God can place in the heart of a believer who has faced and overcome hardship.

How Could Satan Possibly Allow It?

Evil will never triumph in the face of good. All that is required to overcome it is to stay faithful, to stand firm. After the death of Princess Diana, a television producer called Christian author Philip Yancey to get his opinion on the age-old question, "Why did God allow this to happen?" No one in all human history has answered that question satisfactorily. So Yancey decided to turn the question around: "How could Satan possibly allow it?" How could Satan allow Princess Diana to have such a positive influence on millions of people? She made the world pay attention to victims of AIDS, leprosy, and land mines. Since her death, millions of dollars have been donated to her favorite charities in her memory.

And what about that other famous woman who died the same week? Satan allowed this obscure nun, with no wealth or power, to become a powerhouse of compassion to the needy and sick in India. How could Satan have let Mother Teresa happen?

The primary reason evil and tragedy are a shock to our senses is that our lives are so often filled with joy. We become blinded to our blessings. Complacency sets in, and with it, ingratitude. We are not prepared for a downturn in our fortunes. And when that downturn comes, we are tempted to lash out at God, to accuse Him of falling asleep on the job.

This correction notice appeared in the Milton-Freewater, Oregon, *Valley Herald*: "The title of a First Christian Church program in last week's paper was written as 'Our God Resigns.' The actual title is 'Our God Reigns.'"

Our God will never resign. Even though He allows evil to take up residence on this earth, a day will come when He will reclaim the universe for Himself, when evil will have no power over our lives. Until then, we can rest in the assurance that ultimately, the influence of evil pales in comparison to the influence of good.

Consider the amazing things that are happening in South Africa today. The former government's deliberate program of racial oppression resulted in the jailing, harassment, beatings, torture, and murder of hundreds of black South African citizens. Even some white South Africans sympathetic to the cause of integration and equality paid grievously for their beliefs. In 1990, Father Michael Lapsley served as the chaplain to Nelson Mandela's African National Congress in Zimbabwe. He was the victim of a parcel bomb that blew off both his hands and destroyed one eye.

Today, Lapsley can call upon his own pain in his new ministry position as the chaplain at Cape Town's Trauma Centre for Victims of Violence and Torture. Fortunately, Lapsley has not let his injuries embitter him or leave him hopeless. As he says, "The irony is that with no hands and only one eye, I am freer than those who did this to me."

Father Michael Lapsley could have given in to self-pity after suffering his injuries. He could have become bitter. Few people would criticize him for harboring a grudge. Instead, he chooses to use his own experience with suffering to help others. He chooses to live a powerful message of forgiveness and reconciliation in a society filled with anger and hate. He has found freedom, not in retaliating or maintaining the *status quo*, but in choosing to respond in faith.

During World War II, Ralph Hamburger joined the Dutch Resistance in their efforts to hide Jewish refugees from the Nazis. After the war, Ralph emigrated to the United States, and became a Christian. Eventually, he was able to forgive the Nazis.

Ralph began organizing youth mission trips to Germany, where young people were put to work cleaning up the rubble of war and rebuilding towns. Often, they worked alongside German soldiers who were assigned these same jobs. The soldiers were astounded by the kind of love that inspired these young people's work.

But one Nazi soldier repeatedly returned Ralph's kindness with hatred. Daily, Ralph prayed that God would give him love for this man. Finally, Ralph's loving example broke through this soldier's hate, and he gave his life to Christ. That young Nazi soldier became a pastor of a West German church. Ralph Hamburger is godfather to his children.

God did not ask Ralph Hamburger to do anything extraordinary to reach out to the Nazi soldier. He didn't have to climb Mt. Kilimanjaro or donate a kidney to the guy. He just had to demonstrate love to him. That's it. Evil is actually a type of weakness. It is a *reaction* to pain or fear. But love is not a reaction. It is an *action*. It is a choice. For this reason, love has a power that evil lacks.

Good People Making a Difference

Reverend Gardner C. Taylor, former pastor of the 14,000-member Concord Baptist Church of Christ, is one of the most highly respected preachers in the nation. *Christian Century* magazine labeled him the "poet laureate of American Protestantism," and *Time* magazine named him "the dean of the nation's black preachers."

Sadly, in 1994, Gardner Taylor lost his beloved wife of 52 years, Laura Scott Taylor. She was struck down while crossing a city street. But he has clung to his faith in God in spite of his grief.

He tells of one Sunday night during the Depression when all the electricity went out in the church. Everyone got quiet, startled by the sudden darkness. Then, a deacon called out from the back of the church, "Preach on, Preacher, we can still see Jesus in the dark." And that is the truth that all overcomers live by. We can still see Jesus in the dark.

It is this knowledge that gives us hope. And overcoming is nothing more than hope in action. There is no piece of information in this book more important than this: God loves you. He will never forsake you. With God's help, you can take any hurt, limitation, disability, or failure and find good in it. You can heal, you can succeed, you can overcome. God is on your side in this struggle.

> **"I have said this to you, that in Me you may have peace. In the world you have troubles; but be of good cheer, I have overcome the world." — Jesus, found in John 16: 33**

Pastor and author Ron Mehl shares a story he once heard of a certain woman who had devoted her life to following God. In her old age, this woman suffered serious memory loss. Gradually, it stole from her so many cherished memories, it even rendered her incapable of recognizing close friends and family. Yet somehow, she was always able to recall her signature Bible verse, 2 Timothy 1: 12: "For I know whom I have believed, and am persuaded that He is able to keep that which I've committed unto Him against that day." When she could collect no other coherent thought, she could still recite this Bible verse over and over again.

But eventually, age and illness began to chip away at even this precious memory, and she began to lose parts of the verse. Soon she was repeating, "He is able to keep that which I have committed to Him." This snippet of the original verse gave her great comfort. Yet she would lose the ability to recall even those few words. Upon her deathbed, this woman's family noted that she clung to only one word from her favorite verse: "Him." "Him." It was, in the end, all she needed in order to overcome.

Overcomers' Secrets:

1. Believe God has plans to prosper you.
2. Sometimes we must admit we are powerless to overcome on our own.
3. Overcomers share their experience with others.
4. The ultimate act of overcoming involves taking an evil act and creating good out of it.
5. All that is required to overcome evil is to stay faithful, to stand firm.

ENDNOTES

BE PASSIONATE!

Story of Sequoyah on p. 8 from Nancy Caldwell Sorel, *Word People* (New York: American Heritage Press, 1970), pp. 257-259. Story of Clay Whitehurst on p. 9 from Atkinson, Donald. *Celebrating Life* (Nashville: Broadman, 1991), pp. 89-91. All rights reserved. Used by permission. Story of John Searing on p. 10 from Greene, Bob. *He Was A Midwestern Boy On His Own* (New York: Collier MacMillan, 1991), pp. 57-59. Story of Luke Zimmerman on p. 10 from the Associated Press, Prodigy on-line news service. Story of Jan Scruggs on p. 12 from "What Winners Know," condensed from *The Winner Within*, by Pat Riley, *Reader's Digest*, March 1994, p. 178. Story of Lis Hartel on p. 12 from Edwin Muller, "Drama in Real Life: She Rode to Triumph Over Polio," *Reader's Digest*, vol. 67, no. 400, August 1955, pp. 59-62. Found in Marshall, Nancy Thies and Pam Vredevelt, *Women Who Compete* (Old Tappan, N.J.: Fleming H. Revell Co., 1998), pp. 21-26. Story of Cheryl Prewitt Salem on p. 13 from *Storms of Perfection* by Andy Andrews (Lightning Crown Publishers, 1994), pp. 104-106. Story of Mike McIntyre on p. 15 from"The Kindness of Strangers," from the book by Mike McIntyre, *Reader's Digest,* May 1997, pp. 80-84. Story of Linda Finch on p. 15 from"The Sky's the Limit," by Peg Roen, *Aspire,* February/March 1997, pp. 33-34. Story of Norbert Rillieux on p. 16 from"How Black Inventors Changed America," by Kevin Chappell, *Ebony,* February 1997, p. 50. Story of Rich Walsh on p. 16 from Larson, Bruce. *What God Wants To Know* (San Francisco: HarperSanFrancisco, 1993), pp. 31-32. Story of C.T. Studd on p. 18 from Maxwell, John C. *Be a People Person* (Wheaton, Ill.: Victor Books, 1989), p. 145. Story of Rosie O'Donnell on p. 18 from Parish, James Robert. *Rosie: Rosie O'Donnell's Biography* (New York: Carroll & Graf Pub., Inc., 1997), pp. 3, 6-7. Story of Ruth Plymire on p. 19 from"Psalm 85: Starting Over," by George O. Wood, *Pentecostal Evangel,* March 30, 1997, p. 6.

CONFIDENCE FOR DUMMIES

Story of Bill Walsh on p. 21 from "No Hard Feelings," *Lexington Herald-Leader,* May 14, 1997, p. C2. Story of Sylvester Stallone on p. 23 from Plashin, Glenn. *Turning Point* (New York: Carol Publishing Group, 1992), p. 220. Story of Maya Angelou on p. 24 from "Toxic Thoughts Syndrome," by Laura B. Randolph, *Ebony,* September 1998, p. 30. Story of George Lopez on p. 25 from McGinniss, Alan Loy. *Confidence: How to Succeed At Being Yourself* (Minneapolis, Minnesota: Augsburg Publishing House, 1987), pp. 86-88. Used by permission. Thanks to Rev. Bill Akers for these ideas on Gideon. Story of Charles Givens on p. 27 from Givens, Charles J. *SuperSelf:*

Doubling Your Personal Effectiveness (NY: Simon & Schuster, 1993), pp. 31-35. Story of Les Brown on p. 28 from Brown, Les. *Live Your Dreams* (New York: Avon Books, 1992), pp. 62-63. Story of Elton Richardson on p. 28 from "One Step At A Time," by Judith Lynn Howard, *Aspire,* February/ March 1997, pp. 48-50. Story of Elias Howe on p. 30 from Hylander, C. J., *American Inventors* (New York: The Macmillan Company, 1934), pp. 66-72. Story of John Kilcullen on p. 30 from "He's No Dummy," profile of John Kilcullen by Bob Alexander, *Selling Power,* Apr. 1996, pp. 13-16. Story of Elizabeth Kenny on p. 31 from Marlow, Joan. *The Great Women* (New York: Galahad Books, 1979), pp. 259-265. Story of Michelangelo on p. 32 from Barker, Dr. William P. *Tarbell's* (Elgin, Illinois: David C. Cook Church Ministries, 1994).

BUILD YOUR OWN FAN CLUB

Story of Dr. Louis Gonzales on p. 33 from *Mentors, Masters and Mrs. MacGregor,* compiled by Jane Bluestein, Ph.D. (Health Communications, Inc., Deerfield Beach, FL: 1995), pp. 110-111. Story of Kay Cole James on p. 34 from Fellman, Eric. *The Power Behind Positive Thinking* (San Francisco: HarperSanFrancisco, 1996), pp. 21-22. Story of Bette Midler on p. 35 from Late 1980s interview with Bette Midler, in *Hard To Get* by Nancy Collins (New York: Random House, 1990), p. 207. Study on resilience on p. 35 from "The Miracle of Resilience," by Susan Chollar, *American Health,* April 1994, pp. 73-75. Story of Diane Hanny on p. 36 from "Algebra Lesson," by Diane Hanny, *Guideposts,* November 1997, p. 36. Story of Carla McGhee on p. 37 from "A hoop dancer's dream," by Joannie M.Schrof, *U.S. News & World Report,* July 8, 1996, pp. 54-55. Story of Bill Fero on p. 38 from "The Refugee Guests," by Bill Fero, *Guideposts,* May 1997, pp. 20-23. Story of Dave Pelzer on p. 39 from "A Matter of Honor," by Dave Pelzer, from *A 4th Course of Chicken Soup for the Soul* by Jack Canfield, Mark Victor Hansen, Hanoch McCarty, and Meladee McCarty (Deerfield Beach, Florida: Health Communications, Inc., 1997), pp. 161-164. Story of Greg LeMond on p. 40 from "Wheels of Fortune," by Malcolm Fleschner, *Personal Selling Power,* Sept. 1995, pp. 16, 20. Story of Dat Nguyen on p. 41 from "Music Was His Passport," by Anita Bartholomew, *Reader's Digest,* March 1997, p. 41-48. Story of Corrie ten Boom on p. 41 from Ten Boom, Corrie. *Tramp for the Lord* (New York: Jove Books, 1978), pp. 45-46. Cited in Anders, Max. *The Good Life* (Dallas: Word Publishing, 1993), pp. 120-121. Story of Patty and Margaret on p. 43 from "Cable from Kabul: Spartan Samaritan At Large!" by Patty Perrin, *Modern Maturity,* Mar/ Apr 1997, pp. 16, 18.

WHO SAYS?

Story of Sarah Breedlove on p. 45 from Jim Haskins. *One More River to Cross: The Stories of Twelve Black Americans* (New York: Scholastic Inc.,

1992), pp. 14-25. Reprinted by permission of Scholastic, Inc. Story of Francois Huber on p. 48 from Trager, James. *The Food Chronology* (New York: Henry Holt and Company, 1995), p. 185. Study of high achievers on p. 48 from "Energy!" by Gini Kopecky, *American Health*, September 1994, pp. 62, 67. Story of Fanny J. Crosby on p. 48 from *Decision*, December 1997. Story of Winston Churchill on p. 49 from Humes, James C. *The Sir Winston Method* (New York: William Morrow & Company, Inc., 1991), pp, 15-16. Story of Thomas Edison on p. 49 from Hylander, C.J. *American Inventors* (New York: The Macmillan Company, 1934), pp.158-160. Story of R. David Smith on p. 50 from "Local Heroes," *Time,* March 10, 1997, p. 28. Story of Dan Lawrence on p. 50 from "His Voice Touches Thousands," by Michael Ryan, *Parade*, May 11, 1997, pp. 18-19. Story of Julius Caesar on p. 52 from Daniel Cohen. *Great Mistakes* (New York: M. Evans and Co., Inc., 1979), pp. 22-23. Story of George Bush on p. 52 from *Life*, May 1997, p. 25. Story of origin of rugby on p. 53 from *New Encyclopedia of Sports* by Ralph Hickok (New York: McGraw-Hill Book Co., 1977). Story of Three Legs Are Better Than None on p. 53 from "Champion Frog Lives Up to His Name," The Associated Press, Prodigy News Service. Story of Ursula Bacon on p. 55 from *Chocolate for a Woman's Soul* by Kay Allenbaugh (NY: Fireside Books, from Simon & Schuster, 1997), pp. 93-95. Morris Mandel on p. 55 quote from *The Jewish Press*, in the *Catholic Digest*, Nov. '92, p. 195. Story of Georgia Griffith on p. 55 from "Her Keyboard Is a Window to the World," by Barbara Bedway, *Good Housekeeping*, April 1997, p. 28. Story of Mel Borchardt on p. 56 from Schuller, Robert A. *The World's Greatest Comebacks* (Nashville: Thomas Nelson Publishers, 1988), pp. 4-5 and 12-13. This is a paraphrase. Used by permission. Story of Clooney brothers on p. 57 from *Nick: Collected Columns of Nick Clooney*. Printing by The Merten Co., columns from the XStar Radio Network, 1995, pp. 33-35. Story of Bernard Carabello on p. 58 from Rivera, Geraldo. *A Special Kind of Courage* (New York: Simon and Schuster, 1976), pp. 79-109. Story of Helen Keller on p. 59 from Faber, Harold and Doris. *American Heroes Of The 20th Century* (New York: Random House, 1967), pp. 33-35.

TURNING FAILURE INTO ICE CREAM

Story of Mel Tormè on p. 61 from Tormè, Mel. *It Wasn't All Velvet* (New York: Kensington Publishing Company, 1988), pp. 85-86. Story of Karoly Takacs on p. 62 from Wallechinsky, David. *The Complete Book of the Olympics* (Boston: Little, Brown, & Co., 1992), p. 444. Story of Annie Oakley on p. 62 from Morris, Desmond. *The Book of Ages* (New York: The Viking Press, 1983). Story of Ben and Jerry on p. 63 from "Passing the Scoop: Ben & Jerry," by Claudia Dreifus, *The New York Times Magazine*, p. 40. Story of Stephen J. Cannell on p. 64 from Kersey, Cynthia. *Unstoppable* (Naperville, IL:

Sourcebooks, Inc., 1998), pp. 65-68. Story of Edmund McIlhenny on p. 65 from *Illustration Digest*, Jan.-Feb. 1992, p. 12. Story of Fred Kort on p. 66 from "Everything in History Was Against Them," by Carol J. Loomis, *Fortune,* April 13, 1998, pp. 67-72. Story of Paul Gonzales on p. 67 from "Hall of Plucky Heroes," *U.S. News & World Report*, July 15-22, 1996, p. 73. Story of Joseph Sorrentino on p. 68 from George Shinn, *The Miracle Of Motivation* (Wheaton, Illinois: Tyndale House Publishers, Inc., 1981), pp. 120-123. Used by permission of Tyndale House Publishers. Story of Mack Gaston on p. 69 from "Victory At Sea," by Admiral Mack C. Gaston, USN (retired), *Guideposts*, March 1997, pp. 6-8. Story of Booker T. Washington on p. 69 from "'No' to cultural Ebonics," by Marvin Olasky, *World*, Feb. 1, 1997, p. 30. Used by permission. Story of Earl Woods on p. 71 from Woods, Earl, with Pete Daniels. *Training A Tiger: A Father's Guide to Raising a Winner in Both Golf and Life* (New York: HarperCollins Publishers, 1997), xvi-xvii. Story of Vince Robert on p. 72 from Ziglar, Zig. *Ziglar on Selling* (Nashville: Oliver Nelson, 1991), pp. 343-344. Stories of Cal Ripken and Bill Toomey on p. 72 from B. Eugene Griessman, *Time Tactics Of Very Successful People* (New York: McGraw-Hill, Inc., 1994), p. 174. Story of Bjarni Herjolfssen on p. 73 from From *The White Lantern*, by Evan Connell, submitted by Lew Button, Fishertown Community Bible Church, Fishertown Pennsylvania. Found in *parables, etc.*, July 1996, p. 2.

NO "IG NOBEL" AIMS
Story of the Ig Nobels on p. 75 from "The IG Nobel Prize," by Doug Steward, *Omni*, October 1994, p. 24. Story of the Baraka School on p. 76 from "Kenyan school gives U.S. boys new start," by Susan Linnee, Associated Press, *Lexington Herald-Leader*, April 7, 1997, p. A5. Story of Merck & Co. On p. 77 from Carter, Jimmy. *Living Faith* (New York: Random House Large Print, 1996), pp. 189-191. Story of Jimmy Carter on p. 78 from "Guardian Angel," from *Just As I Am* by Billy Graham. HarperCollins, *U.S. News & World Report*, May 5, 1997, p. 66. Story of John McCain on p. 79 from "The Subversive," by Michael Lewis, *The New York Times Magazine*, May 25, 1997, pp. 32, 36-37, 62. Used by permission. Story of Father Carlos and Mama Una on p. 81 from "Castaways in Kigali," by Phillipe Broussard in Le Monde (Paris),*World Press Review*, April 1997, p. 36. Story of Bud Ogle on p. 82 from "100 Things the Church Is Doing Right," segment on Bud Ogle by Philip Yancey, *Christianity Today*, November 17, 1997, pp. 38-39. Used by permission. Story of Celecca Cutts on p. 83 from "Shattered to Share," by Robert J. Morgan, *Moody*, Jul./Aug. 1995, p. 46. Story of Sergeant Richard Kirkland on p. 83 from Lanier, Richard Nunn. *The Angel of Marye's Heights*, in *Before You Call I Will Answer* by David A. Redding (Old Tappan, N. J.: Fleming H. Revell Company, 1985), pp. 141-144. Story of Beulah Mae Donald on p. 84 from "Terror," an interview

with lawyer and activist Morris Dees, by Colonel David H. Hackworth, *Modern Maturity,* Sept./ Oct. 1997, pp. 59-60. Story of Edith Cavell on p. 85 from Donaldson, Norman and Betty. *How Did They Die?* (St. Martin's Mass Market Paper, 1994), p. 63. Story of Joaquin Miller on p. 86 from Watson, Lillian Eichler. *Light From Many Lamps* (New York: Simon & Schuster, Inc., 1951, 1979), pp. 138-140. Story of Estevanico Dorantez on p. 86 from From *Famous Firsts of Black Americans* by Sibyl Hancock (Gretna, La.: Pelican Publishing Company, Inc., 1983), pp. 15-16. Used by permission of the publisher, Pelican Publishing Company, Inc. Raisa Gorbachev quote on p. 87 from Gorbachev, Raisa M. *I Hope* (New York: HarperCollins, 1991), p. 97. From Naylor, Thomas H., William H. Willimon, and Magdalena R. Naylor. *The Search For Meaning* (Nashville: Abingdon Press, 1994), pp. 104-105. Story of Carolyn McCarthy on p. 88 from "My first year in Washington," by Rep. Carolyn McCarthy, *McCall's*, Sept.1997, p. 83. Story of Dianne Clements on p. 88 from "My child didn't have to die!" by Dianne Clements, Katherine Baranski, and Tamara Mechem, as told to Carolyn Holt, *McCall's*, April 1997, pp. 56, 58. Used by permission. Story of "Wake up, Deborah" on p. 89 from "Mothers Movement Awakens Missions," by Debra Fleetwood Wood, *Christianity Today*, May 19, 1997, p.45. Used by permission. Story of Jane Addams on p. 91 from Commager, Henry Steele. *Crusaders For Freedom* (Garden City, New York: Doubleday & Co., Inc., 1962), pp. 101-108. Story of Elizabeth Fry on p. 92 from Deen, Edith. *Great Women Of The Christian Faith* (New York: Harper & Row, Publishers, 1959), pp. 164-170. Story of Mahatma Gandhi on p. 92 from Mosley, Steven R. *Glimpses of God* (Sisters, Oregon: Questar Publishers, Inc., 1990), pp. 83-85. Story of Celine Dion on p. 94 from "Celine Dion's Gift of Love," by Bonnie Siegler, *Good Housekeeping,* February 1997, p. 23.

GETTING BACK ON THE WHEEL
Story of the church on p. 95 by Nancy L. Dorner in *God's Vitamin "C" for the Spirit*, by Kathy Collard Miller and D. Larry Miller (Lancaster, Pennsylvania: Starburst Publishers, 1996), pp. 55-56. Story of Eusebius on p. 97 from William M. Batten, *Fortune.* Story of William Sangster on p. 97 from Wiersbe, Warren. *Wycliffe Handbook of Preaching & Preachers*, p. 215. Story of Kendra Seaman on p. 98 from "Falling off the Wheel," by Dean Nelson, *Herald of Holiness*, March 1997, p. 32. Story of Sir Harry Lauder on p. 98 from Allen, Charles L. *Powerless But Not Helpless* (Tarrytown, NY: Fleming H. Revell Co., 1954/1992). pp. 41-42. Story of Luther Bridgers on p. 98 from Murphree, Jon Tal. *Made To Be Mastered* (Grand Rapids, Mich.: Baker Book House, 1984), pp. 11-12. Story of David on p. 100 from Dickens, Monica. *Miracles of Courage,* out of print, 1985. Story of Orson Vila on p. 100 from *National & International Religion Report*, June 24, 1996, p. 7. Story of Matthew Woodley on p. 102 from "My Second Call to Ministry," by Matthew

Woodley, *Leadership*, Winter 1998, p. 57. Used by permission. Story of Noble Alexander on p. 104 from "Bittersweet Cuban Memories," by John W. Kennedy, *Christianity Today*, January 12, 1998, p. 24. Martin Luther on p. 105 quote from "Caught in the Grip of Fear," by Joe B. Brown, *Moody*, Sept./Oct. 1996, p. 13. Story of Len Burton on p. 105 from Burton, Ben. *The Chicken That Won a Dogfight* (Little Rock, Ark.: August House Publishers, Inc., 1993), pp. 9-10. Story of David Rotherberg on p. 107 from McKechnie, David. *Experiencing God's Pleasure* (Nashville: Oliver Nelson Publishers, 1989). Story of Lou Gehrig on p. 107 from Bennett, William. *The Book of Virtues* (New York: Simon & Schuster, 1993), pp. 496-500. Story of Horatio Spafford on p. 108 from "How To Win Over Worry," by John Edmund Haggai, *Plus*, July/August 1994, pp. 34 -35. Story of Tracey Bailey on p. 110 from "Lesson of a Lifetime," by Tracey Bailey, *Guideposts*, April 1997, pp. 14-17. Story of David Cho on p. 111 from Toler, Stan. *God Has Never Failed Me, But He's Sure Scared Me to Death A Few Times* (Tulsa, Oklahoma: Honor Books, 1995), pp. 47-48. Story of Harold Hughes on p. 111 from Mosley, Steven R. *Glimpses of God* (Sisters, Oregon: Questar Publishers, Inc., 1990), pp. 44-47. Story of grieving man on p. 113 from Larson, Bruce. *The Communicator's Commentary—Luke* (Dallas, TX: Word, Inc., 1983), p. 307. Story of Samuel Shoemaker on p. 113 from Galloway, Dale E. *12 Ways to Develop a Positive Attitude* (Wheaton, IL: Tyndale House, Inc., 1975), pp. 29-30. Story of Henry Francis Lyte on p. 113 from Watson, Lillian Eichler. *Light From Many Lamps* (New York: Simon & Schuster, Inc., 1951, 1979), pp. 36-38. Used by permission. Story of Azim Khamisa and Ples Felix on p. 116 from "I Realized That Change Had To Start With Me," by Michael Ryan, *Parade Magazine*, March 2, 1997, p. 22-23. Story of the Polec family on p. 116 from "The family that said 'No' to hate," by Mary Beth McCauley, *McCall's*, February 1998, pp. 56-62. Used by permission. Story of Princess Diana's death on p. 118 from "A Bad Week in Hell," by Philip Yancey, *Christianity Today*, October 27, 1997, p. 112. Story of typo on p. 118 from *Reader's Digest*, September 1993, p. 53. Story of Father Michael Lapsley on p. 119 from "Will the truth set them free?" by Don L. Boroughs, *U.S. News & World Report*, April 28, 1997, p. 44. Story of Ralph Hamburger on p. 119 from Evans, Colleen Townsend. *Love Is An Everyday Thing* (Carmel, N.Y.: Guideposts, published by special arrangement with Fleming H. Revell Co., 1974), pp. 98-100. Story of Gardner Taylor on p. 120 from "The Pulpit King," by Edward Gilbreath, *Christianity Today*, Dec. 11, 1995, pp. 26-27. Story of dying woman on p. 121 from "A Place of Quiet Rest," by Ron Mehl, *Discipleship Journal*, Issue 99, p. 24. Used by permission.